Etudes

A Rilke Recital

Etudes
A Rilke Recital

translations and commentary by
Art Beck

Shanti Arts Publishing
Brunswick, Maine

Etudes: A Rilke Recital

Published by Shanti Arts Publishing
Interior and cover design by Shanti Arts Designs

Shanti Arts LLC
193 Hillside Road
Brunswick, Maine 04011
shantiarts.com

Cover image: (background) Manuscript of Frederic
Chopin's Etude Op. 10, No. 2 in A minor. Wikimedia
Commons. Public Domain. (foreground) Rainer Maria
Rilke in a studio at the Villa Strohl Fern in Rome in 1904.
Wikimedia Commons. Public Domain. The palace and
gardens of the Villa Strohl Fern were built in the late
nineteenth century by the Alsatian Alfred Wilhelm Strohl
after his exile from his native land soon after the German
occupation in 1870. The Villa is known to have housed
and provided studios for dozens of prominent artists
in the late nineteenth and early twentieth centuries.

ISBN: 978-1-951651-56-5 (softcover)

Library of Congress Control Number: 2020948626

Contents

Acknowledgments

Grateful acknowledgment is made to the editors of the following publications where these poems first appeared:

Rilke. Elysian Press Poetry Series, Chapbook no. 5, 1983.

The Insistent Island. Magra Books, 2019.

the following journals:

Big Bridge
Ezra
Heirs
Invisible City
Jacket
Journal of Poetics Research
The Los Angeles Review of Books
OR
Queen Mob's Tea House
Rattle
Sequoia
Woven Tale Press

A BRIEF INTRODUCTION

I. What These Are and What They Aren't

In the afterword to his 2006 adaptation of the *Sonnets to Orpheus* (simply titled *Orpheus*), the Scots poet Don Paterson spends a good deal of time explaining why his poems are "versions" rather than "translations." One translation obstacle he notes is the rhyme-driven musicality of the Orpheus Sonnets. This is a creative process Rilke also seems to have in mind in a 1921 letter written not long before the Sonnets' composition. His correspondent was a Russian diplomat, but one senses Rilke is commenting primarily to himself:

> Do not say anything against rhyme. It is a mighty goddess indeed, the deity of very secret and very ancient coincidences, and one must never let the fires on its altars burn out. She is extremely temperamental: one can neither anticipate nor invoke her.

In that sense rhyme and musicality (as opposed to mere "versification") are what happens when the hitherto unnoted intent of the poem supplants whatever intent the poet started out with: the spark that transmutes a poem from "words on paper" to a living entity. That process can't be duplicated in poetic translation, except in flat "paint by the numbers" mimicry, without interjecting a new spontaneous combustion that makes its own unique way in the new language. In Paterson's words: "one can no more translate a poem than one can a piece of music."

I'm sympathetic to that view, as was Robert Frost in his "poetry is what gets lost in translation" quip.

But music, after all, can be, and is performed, transposed, adapted, and sung in languages and ways the composer never anticipated. Weill, Brecht, and Lenya's "Mackie Messer" became Louis Armstrong's and Ella Fitzgerald's with no harm to either the German or English language—only enrichment and the sense that the "original" energy lies somewhere beneath all the various versions. There are good and inept musical performances, but the overriding audience criterion of judgment (at least in our informal age) is how they work on their own stage, rather than how they work vis-a-vis the composer's score.

Paterson liberated himself from the Gordian knot dilemma by refusing to use the term "translation" and further distanced himself by adding descriptive titles to Rilke's untitled sonnets. Appropriately, his "versions" were published without the German text.

My approach with this volume is somewhat the opposite. I began translating Rilke in the late 1970s with M. D. Herter Norton's late 1930s near-literal renderings as a resource to guide my entry-level undergraduate German. This was an era when "liberal" trumped "literal" in poetry translation. People like Robert Bly and Robert Lowell were guiding lights as I tried to coax Mrs. Norton's German-faithful lines out of an English that sometimes seemed to flirt with Pennsylvania Dutch. At the time, Rilke's poems (seen darkly through Norton's mirror) seemed missives to a young jazz musician / poet eager to get out of himself and try something new. I was blithely starting out from where Don Paterson seems to have ended after long soul searching.

A number of my Rilke forays were collected in a slim 1983 volume edited by Dana Gioia, a then budding New Formalist, whose back cover blurb nevertheless proudly proclaimed: "Art Beck . . . has recast every poem, violently changing the forms and rhythms." In his view then (and mine), why not?

Were those poems "translations" or "versions" or "adaptations," etc.? That volume called them "performances." And it's a still useful term and concept. In my mind, "performance" doesn't preclude or qualify "translation," rather it helps to explain its possibility.

II. How Did I Get from There to Here?

Most of those 1983 chapbook poems are included in this volume, but in significantly revised form. As I returned to these pieces over the years, it wasn't so much to perfect or polish the English renditions as to listen more closely to the "original score."

Translating poetry is writing poetry, only harder. And the new language inescapably skews as it transplants the original. The problem with that mutation isn't the resonances it adds, but those it forecloses. My multiple look, gradual revisions were much more leisured than my first versions and became primarily an exercise in chipping away superfluities, among them adjectives and images sometimes implied but not stated in the original. Hopefully, they exhibit more appreciation (often with the help of consultation with native speakers) of complexities too easily overlooked by a surface reading. These revisions were a sporadic, largely aimless process until spring of 2004 when I was awarded a month-long residency at Centrum Arts in Port Townsend, Washington. In my application I said I wanted to spend my retreat translating *Sonnets to Orpheus*. To my surprise I managed to work my way through the entire First Part. And as a further personal bonus, I found myself navigating in a serviceable faux-sonnet mode. The translations weren't rhyme-driven, but still reasonably melodic and preserved the sonnet turn. They became facing-page compatible with the originals.

Translating the Second Part of the Orpheus Sonnets took much longer—nearly fifteen years, finally coming to fruition in late 2019 when I realized I only had some ten poems left to translate. Over all this time, I think I became not only a better reader of Rilke, but a more technically adept poet. Both, I think, were the result of taking the time to internalize the poems, the way a pianist's fingers, say, absorb the spontaneity of the score through long repetitive practice.

Are these current versions more accurate or better representations of Rilke's German? That was my intent, but in the process I also grew more appreciative of just how elusive that goal could be with poetry of this depth and resonance. So they remain "performances," perhaps *etudes*, of Rilke. They should be judged by their English, not their German. They are in no way "definitive," but hopefully they're attentive renditions, an attempt at fertile dialogue. In search of that fertility, some may wander, willfully or willingly, to places in English too distant from their roots. I tried to minimize that, but poetry translation, like emigration, is a re-creative act.

PART ONE

SELECTIONS FROM 1902 – 1912

Ende des Herbstes

Ich sehe seit einer Zeit,
wie alles sich verwandelt.
Etwas steht auf und handelt
und tötet und tut Leid.

Von Mal zu Mal sind all
die Gärten nicht dieselben;
von den gilbenden zu der gelben
langsamem Verfall:
wie war der Weg mir weit.

Jetzt bin ich beiden leeren
und schaue durch alle Alleen.
Fast bis zu den fernen Meeren
kann ich den ernsten schweren
verwehrenden Himmel sehn.

End of Autumn

Ever since that once, I've always seen it.
How everything becomes its own defeat.
Some new thing develops, wants to bargain,
then kills and offers its regrets.

And instant by instant all the gardens
are losing hold of themselves, fading
from yellowish to yellow, into a slow
decay. What a long way I've come

to just be so finally empty. To look
down the long avenues almost
to the ocean, look up and see
an utterly grave forbidding sky.

Abend

Der Abend wechselt langsam die Gewänder,
die ihm ein Rand von alten Bäumen hält;
du schaust: und von dir scheiden sich die Länder,
ein himmelfahrendes und eins, das fällt;

und lassen dich, zu keinem ganz gehörend,
nicht ganz so dunkel wie das Haus, das schweigt,
nicht ganz so sicher Ewiges beschwörend
wie das, was Stern wird jede Nacht und steigt–

und lassen dir (unsäglich zu entwirrn)
dein Leben bang und riesenhaft und reifend,
so daß es, bald begrenzt und bald begreifend,
abwechselnd Stein in dir wird und Gestirn.

Evening

changing, ever so slowly, into the vestments
held out for it at the old forest's boundary: As
you watch, the landscapes separate and diverge,
one skyward as the other descends.

You linger, belonging entirely to neither. Not quite
as gray as the house curled up in silence; certainly
not as confident about eternity as the part
that takes nightly flight, into the firmament—

So you're left with (inexpressibly to untangle)
your life, that panicking swollen ripening thing
that seems almost trapped, almost a birth,
sometimes a stone in you, sometimes, star.

Früher Apollo

Wie manches Mal durch das noch unbelaubte
Gezweig ein Morgen durchsieht, der schon ganz
im Frühling ist: so ist in seinem Haupte
nichts, was verhindern könnte, dass der Glanz

aller Gedichte uns fast tödlich träfe;
denn noch kein Schatten ist in seinem Schaun,
zu kühl für Lorbeer sind noch seine Schläfe,
und später erst wird aus den Augenbraun

hochstämmig sich der Rosengarten heben,
aus welchem Blätter, einzeln, ausgelöst
hintreiben werden auf des Mundes Beben,

der jetzt noch still ist, niegebraucht und blinkend
und nur mit seinem Lächeln etwas trinkend,
als würde ihm sein Singen eingeflößt.

Infant Apollo

The way once in a while through the still bare
branches a morning glares through that's already
utter Spring. That's the way there's nothing
in his head to keep the concentrated brilliance

of all poems from almost fatally searing us.
Nothing shields us from his stare. His
temples haven't earned their laurel yet.
And only later would his eyebrows sprout

into a tall rosegarden whose petals
would one by one fall, swirl and float
into a quivering mouth that just yet is

still mute, unused, gleaming, and drinking
only with his smile, something unseen.
As if his songs were being instilled in him.

Östliches Taglied

Ist dieses Bette nicht wie eine Küste,
Ein Küstenstreifen nur, darauf wir liegen?
Nichts ist gewiß als deine hohen Brüste,
Die mein Gefühl in Schwindeln überstiegen.

Denn diese Nacht, in der so vieles schrie,
In der sich Tiere rufen und zerreißen,
Ist sie uns nicht entsetzlich fremd? Und wie:
Was draußen langsam anhebt, Tag geheißen,
Ist das uns denn verständlicher als sie?

Man müßte so sich ineinanderlegen
Wie Blütenblätter um die Staubgefäße:
So sehr ist überall das Ungemäße
Und häuft sich an und stürzt sich uns entgegen.

Doch während wir uns aneinander drücken,
Um nicht zu sehen, wie es ringsum naht,
Kann es aus dir, kann es aus mir sich zücken:
Denn unsre Seelen leben von Verrat.

Dawn Song

Isn't this bed a sort of beach, a cliff-enclosed
strip of coast we've washed up on?
Where nothing's certain but my emotions
trying to dizzily scale your towering breasts.

Because this kind of night—so much was screaming,
animals seemed to call to, then claw one another—
is that so appallingly alien to us? What's slowly
unfurling outside, the thing we've agreed to call
daylight—is it any more comprehensible?

It's a need we have to lie together as
delicately interwoven as petals and stamen.
Until all the unbridled elements overflow
everywhere and cover us in waves.

But even while we squeeze into each
other to wall ourselves around it all,
you desert me, I desert you: Because
our souls live by betrayal

Der Ölbaum-Garten

Er ging hinauf unter dem grauen Laub
ganz grau und aufgelöst im Ölgelände
und legte seine Stirne voller Staub
tief in das Staubigsein der heißen Hände.

Nach allem dies. Und dieses war der Schluß.
Jetzt soll ich gehen, während ich erblinde,
und warum willst Du, daß ich sagen muß
Du seist, wenn ich Dich selber nicht mehr finde.

Ich finde Dich nicht mehr. Nicht in mir, nein.
Nicht in den andern. Nicht in diesem Stein.
Ich finde Dich nicht mehr. Ich bin allein.

Ich bin allein mit aller Menschen Gram,
den ich durch Dich zu lindern unternahm,
der Du nicht bist. O namenlose Scham...

Später erzählte man: ein Engel kam–.

Warum ein Engel? Ach es kam die Nacht
und blätterte gleichgültig in den Bäumen.
Die Jünger rührten sich in ihren Träumen.
Warum ein Engel? Ach es kam die Nacht.

Die Nacht, die kam, war keine ungemeine;
so gehen hunderte vorbei.
Da schlafen Hunde und da liegen Steine.
Ach eine traurige, ach irgendeine,
die wartet, bis es wieder Morgen sei.

The Garden of Olives

He arose and went out under the grey
foliage into the bleak abandoned olive
grove and rested his dusty forehead in his
hot dusty hands. After all of it: This.

Just like this, it's over. I'm departing
utterly blind. And how can You still
ask me to proclaim you exist, when
I no longer find you anywhere?

You're nowhere now. No, not in me.
Nor any of the others. Not even in this stone.
I can't find you anymore. I'm alone.

Alone with the totality of human
grief that I wanted to ease with your name,
You who aren't—what nameless shame . . .

Later, the stories said an angel came . . .

Why an angel? Ah, night came
and riffled idly in the leaves.
The disciples turned in their dreams.
Why an angel? Ah, only night came.

A night that wasn't special, no
different than a hundred others,
where dogs sleep and stones lie
in a night as sad as any that awaits
just another dawn. Because

—*continued*

Denn Engel kommen nicht zu solchen Betern,
und Nächte werden nicht um solche groß.
Die Sich-Verlierenden läßt alles los,
und sie sind preisgegeben von den Vätern
und ausgeschlossen aus der Mütter Schooß.

angels don't answer such prayers
and nights don't offer much help.
The self-forsaken are altogether
forsaken. Left by their fathers to
die, spurned by their mothers' womb.

Pietà

So seh ich, Jesus, deine Füße wieder,
die damals eines Jünglings Füße waren,
da ich sie bang entkleidete und wusch;
wie standen sie verwirrt in meinen Haaren
und wie ein weißes Wild im Dornenbusch.

So seh ich deine niegeliebten Glieder
zum erstenmal in dieser Liebesnacht.
Wir legten uns noch nie zusammen nieder,
und nun wird nur bewundert und gewacht.

Doch, siehe, deine Hände sind zerrissen—:
Geliebter, nicht von mir, von meinen Bissen.
Dein Herz steht offen, und man kann hinein:
das hätte dürfen nur mein Eingang sein.

Nun bist du müde, und dein müder Mund
hat keine Lust zu meinem wehen Munde—.
O Jesus, Jesus, wann war unsre Stunde?
Wie gehn wir beide wunderlich zugrund.

Pietà

So it's like this, Jesus, I see your feet again.
They were a sweet stripling's feet then, when
I nervously undressed them to wash—
the way they stood confused in my hair
like a white deer caught in brambles.

So this is how I see your never caressed naked
limbs for the first time: On this *Liebesnacht*.
We never did lie down together.
Now I can only imagine and wonder.

But look how your hands are torn—
not, darling, by my love bites. Your
heart is pierced for anyone to enter.
The doorway should have been mine, alone.

Now you're exhausted, your slack lips
have no use for my sad mouth. Ah Jesus,
Jesus, when was our appointed hour?
Now both our dreams are wreckage.

Inspired by Rodin's Christ and the Magdelen

Der Panther

Im Jardin des Plantes, Paris

Sein Blick ist vom Vorübergehn der Stäbe
so müd geworden, daß er nichts mehr hält.
Ihm ist, als ob es tausend Stäbe gäbe
und hinter tausend Stäben keine Welt.

Der weiche Gang geschmeidig starker Schritte,
der sich im allerkleinsten Kreise dreht,
ist wie ein Tanz von Kraft um eine Mitte,
in der betäubt ein großer Wille steht.

Nur manchmal schiebt der Vorhang der Pupille
sich lautlos auf –. Dann geht ein Bild hinein,
geht durch der Glieder angespannte Stille –
und hört im Herzen auf zu sein.

The Panther

In the Botanical Garden Zoo, Paris

His eyes glaze, exhausted by the circling
bars, no longer able to focus. He sees
a thousand bars. And no world
beyond those thousand bars.

That clawless dance, those pliant, powerful,
ever tightening steps are like a ritual
of strength around its source. So that
great will can be anesthetized.

Except every so often, it's as if a curtain
in the pupils draws back. Then an image
darts in, tenses its way through his legs
to quietly enter his heart and die.

Vor dem Sommerregen

Auf einmal ist aus allem Grün im Park
Man weiß nicht was, ein Etwas, fortgenommen;
Man fühlt ihn näher an die Fenster kommen
Und schweigsam sein. Inständig nur und stark

Ertönt aus dem Gehölz der Regenpfeifer,
Man denkt an einen Hieronymus:
So sehr steigt irgend Einsamkeit und Eifer
Aus dieser einen Stimme, die der Guß

Erhören wird. Des Saales Wände sind
Mit ihren Bildern von uns fortgetreten,
Als dürften sie nicht hören was wir sagen.

Es spiegeln die verblichenen Tapeten
Das ungewisse Licht von Nachmittagen,
In denen man sich fürchtete als Kind.

Before Summer Rain

All at once—who knows what—but
something's gone out from everything
green in the park. You can feel it: Gathering
closer, silent at the window. In the thicket

a plover pipes, urgent and loud,
reminiscent of some Saint Jerome—
that same melange of loneliness and zeal wrapped
in one voice invoking the downpour to come.

The drawing room walls with their
paintings withdraw from us,
as if they aren't supposed to hear

things we might say, And playing on the faded
tapestry is the same uncertain light of those
afternoons it was so frightening to be a child.

Letzter Abend

Aus dem Besitze Frau Nonnas

Und Nacht und fernes Fahren; denn der Train
des ganzen Heeres zog am Park vorüber.
Er aber hob den Blick vom Clavecin
und spielte noch und sah zu ihr hinüber

beinah wie man in einen Spiegel schaut:
so sehr erfüllt von seinen jungen Zügen
und wissend, wie sie seine Trauer trügen,
schön und verführender bei jedem Laut.

Doch plötzlich wars, als ob sich das verwische:
sie stand wie mühsam in der Fensternische
und hielt des Herzens drängendes Geklopf.

Sein Spiel gab nach. Von draußen wehte Frische.
Und seltsam fremd stand auf dem Spiegeltische
der schwarze Tschako mit dem Totenkopf.

Last Evening

With Frau Nonna's permission

And night and long journey, the entire army
mobilized and beginning to pass just beyond
the park. He raised his eyes from the clavichord,
while he played and looked over at her.

Almost as if he were looking into a mirror
filled with his own young face. Sensing
how she'd mourn him made her more
beautiful and seductive with each note.

But it all suddenly blurred as she forced
herself to the window and stood alone
with her racing heartbeat. An outside

breeze encroached, his fingers stopped.
It stood there stark and alien on the mirror
table: The black shako with its death's-head.

Jugend-Bildnis Meines Vaters

Im Auge Traum. Die Stirn wie in Berührung
mit etwas Fernem. Um den Mund enorm
viel Jugend, ungelächelte Verführung,
und vor der vollen schmückenden Verschnürung
der schlanken adeligen Uniform
der Säbelkorb und beide Hände –, die
abwarten, ruhig, zu nichts hingedrängt.
Und nun fast nicht mehr sichtbar: als ob sie
zuerst, die Fernes greifenden, verschwänden.
Und alles andre mit sich selbst verhängt
und ausgelöscht als ob wir's nicht verständen
und tief aus seiner eignen Tiefe trüb –.

Du schnell vergehendes Daguerreotyp
in meinen langsamer vergehenden Händen.

Portrait of My Young Father

A dreaming eye. The forehead contemplating
something far off. An immensely young
unbelievably seductive mouth. And guarding
the delicate lacings of the full dress aristocratic
uniform, the saber hilt covered by both hands—
resting so calmly, awaiting nothing
But you can hardly make them out. As
if they were the first of him to clutch at
distance and disappear. And all the rest
veiled within himself, hidden in his
incomprehensible muddled depths—

How quickly this brownish photograph is
fading in my more slowly fading hands.

Der König

Der König ist sechzehn Jahre alt.
Sechzehn Jahre und schon der Staat.
Er schaut, wie aus einem Hinterhalt,
vorbei an den Greisen vom Rat

in den Saal hinein und irgendwohin
und fühlt vielleicht nur dies:
an dem schmalen langen harten Kinn
die kalte Kette vom Vlies.

Das Todesurteil vor ihm bleibt
lang ohne Namenszug.
Und sie denken: wie er sich quält.

Sie wüßten, kennten sie ihn genug,
daß er nur langsam bis siebzig zählt
eh er es unterschreibt.

The King

The king is sixteen years old.
Sixteen and already the State.
He stares, as if out of a hunting blind,
past the council of elders at something

or other in the hall beyond them.
Seems intent only on pressing
the cold weave of the official chain
on his bare, thin, protruding chin.

The death warrant lies there. Waiting
for his signature. How he agonizes,
they think. If they knew

enough about him, they'd
know he's only counting slowly
to seventy before he signs it.

Spanische Tänzerin

Wie in der Hand ein Schwefelzündholz, weiß,
eh es zur Flamme kommt, nach allen Seiten
zuckende Zungen streckt –: beginnt im Kreis
naher Beschauer hastig, hell und heiß
ihr runder Tanz sich zuckend auszubreiten.

Und plötzlich ist er Flamme, ganz und gar.

Mit einem Blick entzündet sie ihr Haar
und dreht auf einmal mit gewagter Kunst
ihr ganzes Kleid in diese Feuersbrunst,
aus welcher sich, wie Schlangen die erschrecken,
die nackten Arme wach und klappernd strecken.

Und dann: als würde ihr das Feuer knapp,
nimmt sie es ganz zusamm und wirft es ab
sehr herrisch, mit hochmütiger Gebärde
und schaut: da liegt es rasend auf der Erde
und flammt noch immer und ergiebt sich nicht –.
Doch sieghaft, sicher und mit einem süßen
grüßenden Lächeln hebt sie ihr Gesicht
und stampft es aus mit kleinen Füßen.

Spanish Dancer

The way a sulfur match, cupped in the hand, whitens
before it flames, licks out in every direction:
within the intent ring of watching eyes,
the quick, bright heat of her circling
feet shivers until it flares.

And suddenly, he and the dance are altogether fire.

With a blink, she ignites her hair,
then instantly with seductive mastery,
whirls her entire dress into the bonfire
from which her naked arms rear
up like startled rattlesnakes.

As the fire finally clings to her like a slip,
she strips it off completely, aristocratically tosses
it aside with a haughty shrug. And watches:
There it lies, smoldering on the ground, still
burning and unwilling to surrender. And with
a smile on her face and a sweet "hello", she
stamps it out with small, sure steps.

Paris, 1906

Orpheus, Eurydike, Hermes

Das war der Seelen wunderliches Bergwerk.
Wie stille Silbererze gingen sie
als Adern durch sein Dunkel. Zwischen Wurzeln
entsprang das Blut, das fortgeht zu den Menschen,
und schwer wie Porphyr sah es aus im Dunkel.
Sonst war nichts Rotes.

Felsen waren da
und wesenlose Wälder. Brücken über Leeres
und jener große graue blinde Teich,
der über seinem fernen Grunde hing
wie Regenhimmel über einer Landschaft.
Und zwischen Wiesen, sanft und voller Langmut,
erschien des einen Weges blasser Streifen,
wie eine lange Bleiche hingelegt.

Und dieses einen Weges kamen sie.

Voran der schlanke Mann im blauen Mantel,
der stumm und ungeduldig vor sich aussah.
Ohne zu kauen fraß sein Schritt den Weg
in großen Bissen; seine Hände hingen
schwer und verschlossen aus dem Fall der Falten
und wußten nicht mehr von der leichten Leier,
die in die Linke eingewachsen war
wie Rosenranken in den Ast des Ölbaums.
Und seine Sinne waren wie entzweit:
indes der Blick ihm wie ein Hund vorauslief,
umkehrte, kam und immer wieder weit
und wartend an der nächsten Wendung stand, –
blieb sein Gehör wie ein Geruch zurück.

Orpheus, Eurydice, Hermes

Imagine a mineshaft of souls
running as silently through the dark
as silver veins flow. And blood welling
among the roots, on its route to humanity,
clotting like porphyry in the shadows.
Other than this—nothing was red.

There were boulders,
spectral forests, bridges over emptiness,
and the great grey blind pool
suspended over its depths
like rain clouds over a landscape.
And out of these meadows, a vague strip
of trail, gently and patiently, unwound
like a long, pale bandage.

And this is the path they traveled.

Ahead, the thin man in the blue mantle,
silent and anxious, staring straight ahead.
His stride gobbling up the path with big,
unchewed bites, his fists hanging clenched
and heavy from the folds of his falling cloak.
He could no longer comprehend the effortless lyre,
that had grown around his left arm like a rose
vine in the branches of an olive tree.
It was as if his senses were cut in two.
His eyesight ran ahead of him like a dog that
turns around, comes back and runs away again
to stand guard at the next blind turn—
while his hearing lingered like a scent.

—continued

Manchmal erschien es ihm als reichte es
bis an das Gehen jener beiden andern,
die folgen sollten diesen ganzen Aufstieg.
Dann wieder wars nur seines Steigens Nachklang
und seines Mantels Wind was hinter ihm war.
Er aber sagte sich, sie kämen doch;
sagte es laut und hörte sich verhallen.
Sie kämen doch, nur wärens zwei
die furchtbar leise gingen. Dürfte er
sich einmal wenden (wäre das Zurückschaun
nicht die Zersetzung dieses ganzen Werkes,
das erst vollbracht wird), müßte er sie sehen,
die beiden Leisen, die ihm schweigend nachgehn:

Den Gott des Ganges und der weiten Botschaft,
die Reisehaube über hellen Augen,
den schlanken Stab hertragend vor dem Leibe
und flügelschlagend an den Fußgelenken;
und seiner linken Hand gegeben: sie.

Die So-geliebte, daß aus einer Leier
mehr Klage kam als je aus Klagefrauen;
daß eine Welt aus Klage ward, in der
alles noch einmal da war: Wald und Tal
und Weg und Ortschaft, Feld und Fluß und Tier;
und daß um diese Klage-Welt, ganz so
wie um die andre Erde, eine Sonne
und ein gestirnter stiller Himmel ging,
ein Klage-Himmel mit entstellten Sternen –:
Diese So-geliebte.

Sometimes it seemed to reach back to travel
with those other two who were supposed
to be following this entire ascension.
Then, again, it was only his climb's after-ring
and the wind in his cloak that followed him.
And he assured himself: Yes, they're coming.
Said it out loud and heard it echo. Yes.
They were coming. Only how could two people
move without sound? If he could permit himself—
and wouldn't just that one backward look
wreck the entire creation, so close to completion?
—to turn just once, he would certainly see them,
the two weightless beings, who quietly followed him:

That god of errands and messages from afar,
the traveling hood covering his brilliant eyes,
the thin rod held out in front of his body,
wings beating above his heels,
and his left hand held out to—*Her.*

The one so beloved that from one lyre
more grief came than from all grieving-women,
so that a whole world was made of grief
and everything was re-created:
Forest and valley and road and village,
field and river and beast.
And around this other world,
another sun traveled through a star-filled
silent sky. A grieving sky with grimacing stars.
She was so beloved.

—continued

Sie aber ging an jenes Gottes Hand,
den Schrittbeschränkt von langen Leichenbändern,
unsicher, sanft und ohne Ungeduld.
Sie war in sich, wie Eine hoher Hoffnung,
und dachte nicht des Mannes, der voranging,
und nicht des Weges, der ins Leben aufstieg.
Sie war in sich. Und ihr Gestorbensein
erfüllte sie wie Fülle.
Wie eine Frucht von Süßigkeit und Dunkel,
so war sie voll von ihrem großen Tode,
der also neu war, daß sie nichts begriff.

Sie war in einem neuen Mädchentum
und unberührbar; ihr Geschlecht war zu
wie eine junge Blume gegen Abend,
und ihre Hände waren der Vermählung
so sehr entwöhnt, daß selbst des leichten Gottes
unendlich leise, leitende Berührung
sie kränkte wie zu sehr Vertraulichkeit.

Sie war schon nicht mehr diese blonde Frau,
die in des Dichters Liedern manchmal anklang,
nicht mehr des breiten Bettes Duft und Eiland
und jenes Mannes Eigentum nicht mehr.

Sie war schon aufgelöst wie langes Haar
und hingegeben wie gefallner Regen
und ausgeteilt wie hundertfacher Vorrat.

Sie war schon Wurzel.

But, now, she went on the arm of the god,
her pace impeded by the long burial shroud,
uncertain, meek and with no impatience.
She was self contained, like someone with higher hopes,
and didn't think about the man who walked ahead
or the path, that climbed back into life.
She was self contained. And being dead
enriched her like a treasure.
Like a fruit full of dark sugar, she was filled
with a death so immense and new
she couldn't quite grasp her role in it.

She'd come into a new childhood
and must not be touched. Her sex
had closed like a young flower at evening,
and her fingertips were so weaned from marriage
that even the gentle god's, infinitely gentle,
guiding hand sickened her with unwelcome intimacy.

She was now, no longer that blonde wife
who in the poet's song once rang and rang.
No longer the wide bed's perfumed and blessed
isle. That man's property, no longer.

She had already come undone like long hair,
had been surrendered like a rainfall,
given away in a hundred portions.

She was root now.

—continued

Und als plötzlich jäh
der Gott sie anhielt und mit Schmerz im Ausruf
die Worte sprach: Er hat sich umgewendet –,
begriff sie nichts und sagte leise: Wer?

Fern aber, dunkel vor dem klaren Ausgang,
stand irgend jemand, dessen Angesicht
nicht zu erkennen war. Er stand und sah,
wie auf dem Streifen eines Wiesenpfades
mit trauervollem Blick der Gott der Botschaft
sich schweigend wandte, der Gestalt zu folgen,
die schon zurückging dieses selben Weges,
den Schritt beschränkt von langen Leichenbändern,
unsicher, sanft und ohne Ungeduld.

And when suddenly, abruptly,
the god stopped her—and sadly exclaimed
the surprising words: He's turned around.
She didn't comprehend, just quietly asked: *Who?*

But some way off, dark in the clear exit,
someone—it could have been anyone—stood,
the one whose face could no longer be recognized.
He stood and watched how on a strip of meadowpath
with a sorrowful expression, the god of messages
silently turned to follow the retreating shape,
her pace impeded by the long burial shroud,
uncertain, meek and without impatience.

Archaïscher Torso Apollos

Wir kannten nicht sein unerhörtes Haupt,
darin die Augenäpfel reiften. Aber
sein Torso glüht noch wie ein Kandelaber,
in dem sein Schauen, nur zurückgeschraubt,

sich hält und glänzt. Sonst könnte nicht der Bug,
der Brust dich blenden, und im leisen Drehen
der Lenden könnte nicht ein Lächeln gehen
zu jener Mitte, die die Zeugung trug.

Sonst stünde dieser Stein entstellt und kurz
unter der Schultern durchsichtigem Sturz
und flimmerte nicht so wie Raubtierfelle

und bräche nicht aus allen seinen Rändern
aus wie ein Stern: denn da ist keine Stelle,
die dich nicht sieht. Du mußt dein Leben ändern.

Archaic Torso of Apollo

We didn't grasp that outrageous head, the eyes
whose irises actually flowered. But his torso
still stares like a chandelier turned low,
dimmed to illuminate just its own steady

flame. Why else would the crease
of the chest muscles blind you? And the slight
tensing of the loin—it's nothing if not a smile
traveling to his center on a journey to procreation.

If not, this would only be a fragment
of mutilated stone under the shoulders' transparent
slump. Wouldn't glisten, anymore than a predator's

fur, or leap like radiating star fire.
Because there isn't any single part of it that isn't
watching you. You have to live another life.

Klage Um Antinous

Keiner begriff mir von euch den bithynischen Knaben,
(daß ihr den Strom anfaßtet und von ihm hübt...)
Ich verwöhnte ihn zwar. Und dennoch: wir haben
ihn nur mit Schwere erfüllt und für immer getrübt.

Wer vermag denn zu lieben? Wer kann es?–Noch keiner.
Und so hab ich unendliches Weh getan–.
Nun ist er am Nil der stillenden Götter einer,
und ich weiß kaum welcher und kann ihm nicht nahn.

Und ihr warfet ihn noch, Wahnsinnige, bis in die Sterne,
da mit ich euch rufe und dränge: meint ihr den?
Was ist er nicht einfach ein Toter? Er wäre es gerne.
Und vielleicht wäre ihm nichts geschehn.

(The Emperor Hadrian's) Lament for Antinous

No one could fathom the Bithynian boy (If only they could
have caught and pulled him from those currents . . .)
I indulgled him to a fault. And yet: We just
smothered him with constant gloom.

Who can master love? Who? No one I've ever
known. All I caused was grief on end. Now he's one
of those nurturing Nile gods—I can hardly tell one from
another—whose presence I'm not allowed in

Insanely, they're launching him to the stars.
Even while I mutter "are you serious?" Can't he
just simply be mortal? He wouldn't have cared.
And maybe none of this would need to be.

Kreuzigung

Längst geübt, zum kahlen Galgenplatze
irgend ein Gesindel hinzudrängen,
ließen sich die schweren Knechte hängen,
dann und wann nur eine große Fratze

kehrend nach den abgetanen Drein.
Aber oben war das schlechte Henkern
rasch getan; und nach dem Fertigsein
ließen sich die freien Männer schlenkern.

Bis der eine (fleckig wie ein Selcher)
sagte: Hauptmann, dieser hat geschrien.
Und der Hauptmann sah vom Pferde: Welcher?
und es war ihm selbst, er hätte ihn

den Elia rufen hören. Alle
waren zuzuschauen voller Lust,
und sie hielten, daß er nicht verfalle,
gierig ihm die ganze Essiggalle
an sein schwindendes Gehust.

Denn sie hofften noch ein ganzes Spiel
und vielleicht den kommenden Elia.
Aber hinten ferne schrie Maria,
und er selber brüllte und verfiel.

Crucifixion

Inured as they were to the routine
of dragging riff-raff to the bald gallows
hill, the sturdy work crew hung around, now
and then flashing big grins at the three

they'd finished off. But the clumsy
executions so quickly accomplished
loomed over the men as if, they too,
dangled like appendages in their leisure.

Until one (bloodstained as a hog butcher)
said: Captain, that one just screamed
something. And the captain, looking
from his horse: Which? Because it seemed

to him he'd also had heard a call: *Elijah*.
All of them were happy to watch. And
to prolong his failure, they sponged
his rattling cough with vinegar.

Because they hoped there was still
some fun to come, maybe even Elijah.
Then some ways off, Mary screamed, and
the one in question howled and failed.

Der Auferstandene

Er vermochte niemals bis zuletzt
ihr zu weigern oder abzuneinen,
daß sie ihrer Liebe sich berühme;
und sie sank ans Kreuz in dem Kostüme
eines Schmerzes, welches ganz besetzt
war mit ihrer Liebe größten Steinen.

Aber da sie dann, um ihn zu salben,
an das Grab kam, Tränen im Gesicht,
war er auferstanden ihrethalben,
daß er seliger ihr sage: Nicht –

Sie begriff es erst in ihrer Höhle,
wie er ihr, gestärkt durch seinen Tod,
endlich das Erleichternde der Öle
und des Rührens Vorgefühl verbot,

um aus ihr die Liebende zu formen
die sich nicht mehr zum Geliebten neigt,
weil sie, hingerissen von enormen
Stürmen, seine Stimme übersteigt.

The Risen

He never, to the very end, refused
their love or denied her showy pride.
And she collapsed under the cross
in a gown of pain bejeweled with that
love's most precious stones.

But then at the grave, when
she came in tears to anoint him,
only to find him risen just for her,
he beatifically told her: No—

Only in their cave did she see
how, strengthened by his death,
he finally forbade her the comforting
oil's anticipated touch to mold

from her the lover who no longer
bends to her beloved because
borne by enormous storms
she soars beyond his voice.

Die Bettler

Du wußtest nicht, was den Haufen
ausmacht. Ein Fremder fand
Bettler darin. Sie verkaufen
das Hohle aus ihrer Hand.

Sie zeigen dem Hergereisten
ihren Mund voll Mist,
und er darf (er kann es sich leisten)
sehn, wie ihr Aussatz frißt.

Es zergeht in ihren zerrührten
Augen sein fremdes Gesicht;
und sie freuen sich des Verführten
und speien, wenn er spricht.

The Beggars

You didn't realize what that gang
was made of. A stranger who
stumbled on beggars peddling
the palms of their hands there.

They show off their rotten
mouths to the traveler to let
him see (since he can afford it)
how leprosy eats them away.

But his foreigner's face collapses
right in front of their ruined eyes.
And they spit as he tries
to say something.

Leichen-Wäsche

Sie hatten sich an ihn gewöhnt. Doch als
die Küchenlampe kam und unruhig brannte
im dunkeln Luftzug, war der Unbekannte
ganz unbekannt. Sie wuschen seinen Hals,

und da sie nichts von seinem Schicksal wußten,
so logen sie ein anderes zusamm,
fortwährend waschend. Eine mußte husten
und ließ solang den schweren Essigschwamm

auf dem Gesicht. Da gab es eine Pause
auch für die zweite. Aus der harten Bürste
klopften die Tropfen; während seine grause
gekrampfte Hand dem ganzen Hause
beweisen wollte, daß ihn nicht mehr dürste.

Und er bewies. Sie nahmen wie betreten
eiliger jetzt mit einem kurzen Huster
die Arbeit auf, so daß an den Tapeten
ihr krummer Schatten in dem stummen Muster

sich wand und wälzte wie in einem Netze,
bis daß die Waschenden zu Ende kamen.
Die Nacht im vorhanglosen Fensterrahmen
war rücksichtslos. Und einer ohne Namen
lag bar und reinlich da und gab Gesetze.

Corpse Washing

They'd grown accustomed to him. Until
they lit the kitchen lamp and it began to flicker
restlessly in the twilight draft. Then the stranger
became utterly strange. They started with his

neck, and since they knew nothing of his story
they cooked one up for him between them
while they washed. The one had a hacking spasm
and left her big vinegar soaked sponge lying

on his face. The other rested a bit, her
stiff bath brush dripping. While his
gruesome cramped hand tried so very
hard to make everyone see
he no longer had a thirst.

And he made his point. With short,
embarrassed coughs they resumed their
work in earnest, while on the wallpaper
their twisting shadows in a silent pattern

flipped and flailed as if in a net. Until at
last the ablution was finished. Gathering
at the uncurtained window, night was
uninterested. As someone nameless lay
there, naked and clean: and decreed.

Auswanderer-Schiff

Neapel

Denk daß einer heiß und glühend flüchte,
und die Sieger wären hinterher,
und auf einmal machte der
Flüchtende kurz, unerwartet, kehr
gegen Hunderte –: so sehr
warf sich das Erglühende der Früchte
immer wieder an das blaue Meer,

als das langsame Orangenboot
sie vorübertrug bis an das große
graue Schiff, zu dem, von Stoß zu Stoße,
andre Boote Fische hoben, Brot, –
während es, voll Hohn, in seinem Schoße
Kohlen aufnahm, offen wie der Tod.

Emigrant-Ship

Naples

Think of sweltering heat and someone
feverishly fleeing. The victors close behind.
Suddenly the fugitive stops short and
turns to face a throng of hundreds—That was
how the fervid radiance of the fruit flashed
out again and again against the blue sea as

the sluggish orange-boat carried them past
to the huge gray ship where bobbing
boats raised loads of fish, bread . . . while
she haughtily filled her belly with
coal, wide open as death.

Die erste Elegie (1912)

Wer, wenn ich schriee, hörte mich denn aus der Engel
Ordnungen? und gesetzt selbst, es nähme
einer mich plötzlich ans Herz: ich verginge von seinem
stärkeren Dasein. Denn das Schöne ist nichts
als des Schrecklichen Anfang, den wir noch grade ertragen,
und wir bewundern es so, weil es gelassen verschmäht,
uns zu zerstören. Ein jeder Engel ist schrecklich.

Und so verhalt ich mich denn und verschlucke den Lockruf

dunkelen Schluchzens. Ach, wen vermögen
wir denn zu brauchen? Engel nicht, Menschen nicht,
und die findigen Tiere merken es schon,
daß wir nicht sehr verläßlich zu Haus sind
in der gedeuteten Welt. Es bleibt uns vielleicht
irgend ein Baum an dem Abhang, daß wir ihn täglich
wiedersähen; es bleibt uns die Straße von gestern
und das verzogene Treusein einer Gewohnheit,
der es bei uns gefiel, und so blieb sie und ging nicht.

O und die Nacht, die Nacht, wenn der Wind voller Weltraum

uns am Angesicht zehrt, wem bliebe sie nicht, die ersehnte,
sanft enttäuschende, welche dem einzelnen Herzen
mühsam bevorsteht. Ist sie den Liebenden leichter?
Ach, sie verdecken sich nur mit einander ihr Los.

Weißt du's *noch* nicht? Wirf aus den Armen die Leere

zu den Räumen hinzu, die wir atmen; vielleicht daß die Vögel
die erweiterte Luft fühlen mit innigerm Flug.

The First Elegy

Then even if I screamed to high heaven, who'd listen
to me there among the angelic orders? And
suppose one of them did swoop me to heart:
I'd die, seared by exposure to that stark, concentrated
being. Because beauty's nothing, the mere beginning
of a panic we're still just barely able to contain.
And we continually praise it, hoping it continues
to disdainfully refrain from obliterating us.
Every one of the angels is horrifying.

So I behave myself and swallow back
the bird call of my dark sobs. Ah—who
can do anything to help it? Not angels. Not
people. And the cunning animals immediately
notice the world's a language in which
we're not always quite at home.
So, for us, what remains? Maybe some tree
or other on the hillside we look at every day,
over and over. Memory lane remains for us,
and the spoiled loyalty of a childish habit
that remains because it enjoys it here
too much to leave. Oh—and night.

Night, when the wind full of outer space
feeds on our faces—well who wouldn't she

stick around for?—longed for, gently disappointed
night, who the solitary heart so painstakingly approaches?
Is she easier on lovers? Or do they
just cover their bets with each other?

Ja, die Frühlinge brauchten dich wohl. Es muteten manche
Sterne dir zu, daß du sie spürtest. Es hob
sich eine Woge heran im Vergangenen, oder
da du vorüberkamst am geöffneten Fenster,
gab eine Geige sich hin. Das alles war Auftrag.
Aber bewältigtest du's? Warst du nicht immer
noch von Erwartung zerstreut, als kündigte alles
eine Geliebte dir an? (Wo willst du sie bergen,
da doch die großen fremden Gedanken bei dir
aus und ein gehn und öfters bleiben bei Nacht.)
Sehnt es dich aber, so singe die Liebenden; lange
noch nicht unsterblich genug ist ihr berühmtes Gefühl.
Jene, du neidest sie fast, Verlassenen, die du
so viel liebender fandst als die Gestillten. Beginn
immer von neuem die nie zu erreichende Preisung;
denk: es erhält sich der Held, selbst der Untergang war ihm
nur ein Vorwand, zu sein: seine letzte Geburt.
Aber die Liebenden nimmt die erschöpfte Natur
in sich zurück, als wären nicht zweimal die Kräfte,
dieses zu leisten. Hast du der Gaspara Stampa
denn genügend gedacht, daß irgend ein Mädchen,
dem der Geliebte entging, am gesteigerten Beispiel
dieser Liebenden fühlt: daß ich würde wie sie?
Sollen nicht endlich uns diese ältesten Schmerzen
fruchtbarer werden? Ist es nicht Zeit, daß wir liebend
uns vom Geliebten befrein und es bebend bestehn:
wie der Pfeil die Sehne besteht, um gesammelt im Absprung
mehr zu sein als er selbst. Denn Bleiben ist nirgends.

Stimmen, Stimmen. Höre, mein Herz, wie sonst nur
Heilige hörten: daß sie der riesige Ruf
aufhob vom Boden; sie aber knieten,
Unmögliche, weiter und achtetens nicht:

Haven't you learned anything after all this time?
Fling the emptiness out of your arms, add it
to the wide open spaces we breathe. Maybe
the expanded breeze will touch the birds
more intimately in their flight.

Sure, spring certainly needed you. All manner
of stars appeared to you and introduced themselves.
The past used to bellow up in waves for you;
and, when you passed an open window, fiddles
surrendered themselves to you. All this was a mission.
But did you accomplish it? Didn't you always
and again, dissipate with expectation, as if everything
would be canceled by a lover arriving?
(Where would you hide her now, with all those strange
reveries that constantly come and go at your place
and so often stay the night?) And if you persist in yearning,
then go on and sing about the loving ones. Their own
celebrated feelings really aren't capable of immortalizing
themselves. Those—you envy them, almost—deserted lovers,
whom you found so much more loving than the satisfied.
Begin the always new and never attainable ode. Think
about it: The hero preserves himself, even his ruin is personal
and foreordained—his own, ultimate real birth. But as for lovers,
exhausted nature just takes them back into her dreamy self
as though she hadn't the strength to do it twice.
Do you really think you've commemorated Gaspara Stampa
properly—so that any young girl whose lover's left her
would compare her feelings to Gaspara's intense poems
and think: "I want to be just like her."? Shouldn't these
oldest pains finally become more productive? It is
time—isn't it?—to lovingly liberate ourselves from our
lovers and shiver and endure it. The way the arrow

So waren sie hörend. Nicht, daß du *Gottes* ertrügest
die Stimme, bei weitem. Aber das Wehende höre,
die ununterbrochene Nachricht, die aus Stille sich bildet.
Es rauscht jetzt von jenen jungen Toten zu dir.
Wo immer du eintratst, redete nicht in Kirchen
zu Rom und Neapel ruhig ihr Schicksal dich an?
Oder es trug eine Inschrift sich erhaben dir auf,
wie neulich die Tafel in Santa Maria Formosa.
Was sie mir wollen? leise soll ich des Unrechts
Anschein abtun, der ihrer Geister
reine Bewegung manchmal ein wenig behindert.

Freilich ist es seltsam, die Erde nicht mehr zu bewohnen,
kaum erlernte Gebräuche nicht mehr zu üben,
Rosen, und andern eigens versprechenden Dingen
nicht die Bedeutung menschlicher Zukunft zu geben;
das, was man war in unendlich ängstlichen Händen,
nicht mehr zu sein, und selbst den eigenen Namen
wegzulassen wie ein zerbrochenes Spielzeug.
Seltsam, die Wünsche nicht weiter zu wünschen. Seltsam,
alles, was sich bezog, so lose im Raume
flattern zu sehen. Und das Totsein ist mühsam
und voller Nachholn, daß man allmählich ein wenig
Ewigkeit spürt. Aber Lebendige machen
alle den Fehler, daß sie zu stark unterscheiden.
Engel (sagt man) wüßten oft nicht, ob sie unter
Lebenden gehn oder Toten. Die ewige Strömung
reißt durch beide Bereiche alle Alter
immer mit sich und übertönt sie in beiden.

trembles on the tightening bow string, collecting in its leap,
more to itself than its self. Because staying here is nowhere.

Voices. Voices. Listen my heart, as only the saints
listened: so that the giant summons lifted them off the ground.
But they still knelt in the air, those impossibles. Furthermore,
they didn't even notice. They were listening so intently.
Not that you could stand the voice of God, by far.
But do you hear the wind-like, incessant message that's
taking shape from the silence? Now, it comes rustling,
rushing to you again from those dead youths. Those times
you deigned to make a visit—wasn't it in the churches, in Rome
and in Naples, that their thwarted destinies quietly touched
you? Or an inscription copied itself on you like an exalted
burden, the way just lately that plaque in Santa Maria Formosa.
What do they want from me?

To gently remove the speck of injured illusion that sometimes,
just a little bit—impedes their spirits' transparent progress.

It's certainly strange to no longer occupy space in this world.
To stop practicing customs you've barely learned.
Not to give roses and other particularly portentous
things the significance of a human future.
For someone once held in endlessly apprehensive
hands—to no longer exist, even your very own name
tossed aside like a broken toy. Strange to no longer want
your wants. Strange to see everything coherent fluttering
loose around the room this way. And death's
a laborious pastime, full of catching up, until only gradually,
you begin to feel the slightest hint of eternity.

Schließlich brauchen sie uns nicht mehr, die Früheentrückten,
man entwöhnt sich des Irdischen sanft, wie man den Brüsten
milde der Mutter entwächst. Aber wir, die so große
Geheimnisse brauchen, denen aus Trauer so oft
seliger Fortschritt entspringt –: *könnten* wir sein ohne sie?
Ist die Sage umsonst, daß einst in der Klage um Linos
wagende erste Musik dürre Erstarrung durchdrang;
daß erst im erschrockenen Raum, dem ein beinah göttlicher
    Jüngling
plötzlich für immer enttrat, das Leere in jene
Schwingung geriet, die uns jetzt hinreißt und tröstet und hilft.

But the living all make the same mistake, they draw
too sharp a distinction for themselves. Angels
(it's said) often don't know whether they're traveling
among the living or the dead. The eternal current
rushes through both countries constantly, drowning
out all differences, pulling every age along.
When all's said and done, those taken before their time
don't need us. They simply wean themselves from mortal
earth the way one outgrows a mother's soft breasts.
But we, who need such big mysteries—for whom,
from sorrows like this, beatific progress so often
wells up—could we live without *them*?
Is the old myth meaningless? The one in which
once upon a time in the lamentation over Linos
the first music ventured out and pushed its way
through the numb shock in that terrified room
the nearly divine youth had suddenly escaped
from forever. And for the first time
shattered the void with that vibration
which, to this day still, ravishes, consoles and helps.

PART TWO

SONNETS TO ORPHEUS, 1922

The first portion of this selection draws largely on *New Poems*, published in 1907 and 1908. Those two volumes seem firmly "modern," arguably a decade ahead in thrust to modernist English language poetry in the last century's first decade. While mostly rhymed with many sonnets included, the strength of *New Poems* is freshness and power of imagery. But they also don't break sharply with, but rather almost come to fruition, with the late nineteenth century. So, the translator is faced with choices of "voice." Does one look backward or forward? Those choices are discussed at length in my afterword, "And Yet Another Archaic Torso—Why?"

While the *New Poems* stake out "modern" territory, Rilke abruptly sidesteps in 1912 with a sense of unease into the "First Duino Elegy," a wandering internal dialogue that seems to foreshadow the existential travail just a few years down the new century's road. The (ultimately ten) *Duino Elegies* leave the concrete world of "thing poems" inspired by Rilke's Paris stay with Rodin and explore what might be characterized as an inner metaphysics of language. Or, in the words of Rilke's biographer, Wolfgang Leppmann: an "attempt to wrest meaning from the human condition in a time little given to faith in God or a belief in the beyond." But apart from their philosophic forays, they're also read for their flashes of what Marina Tsvetaeva described, in a flirtatious 1926 letter to Rilke, as poetic "lightning on lightning."

The *Elegies* would continue, off and on, until early 1922 when in a rush of energized inspiration, Rilke completed the last five, many from notes and fragments that had been germinating since a hiatus in 1915.

Out of the relaxation that followed, *Sonnets to Orpheus* welled up, seemingly from nowhere. From a formal standpoint, they might be described as "sonnets set free." Perhaps it's worth remembering that Rilke whipped out the fifty-five sonnets to Orpheus in what he claimed was a two-week space. It's obvious he wasn't writing into but out of the form—the way Charlie Parker might roll out chorus after chorus of the blues. I use Parker as an example, rather than someone more traditional, say Jimmy Rushing, because in the Orpheus sequence I think Rilke stood the traditional sonnet on its head.

The Shakespearean sonnet in English often takes on an almost geometric progression leading to a "closed conclusion." The sonnets to Orpheus tend instead to take flight and end with harmonic ambiguities and open statements. It's worth noting, I think, that when Rilke returned to the sonnet form for this late-in-life sequence, he said he wanted an "open," "conjugated" sonnet, i.e. something both akin to and yet not a traditional sonnet. He retains the sonnet rhyme schemes, but plays with meter, line breaks and enjambments, varying the presentation from poem to poem. To quote Wolfgang Leppmann:

> The playful impression of the whole cycle, the *Sonnets* minuet measure in contrast to the funeral march presented by the *Elegies*, is a consequence of Rilke's sovereign treatment of the form. In the letter he enclosed . . . for typesetting, he speaks of "the specific challenge and obligation" he had perceived in, "modulating the sonnet, lightening it, carrying it at a run, as it were, without destroying it."

Leppmann also observes that one effect of all this variation is to make the sonnets easily readable in one sitting as a sequence. And I think this is how they're best experienced, as a wandering piece of music with various crescendos, diminuendos, pauses, and arias. If the translation issues of *New Poems* seem mainly "visual," those of *Sonnets to Orpheus* might be characterized as "aural." Their frequent ambiguities are, I think, often due to the subordination of imagery to sonority. To use an analogy with music, it's as if the melody line becomes subordinate to its harmonic roots.

When successful, this "blur" of imagery and sound can also create the sense of a discrete, living object, the obverse perhaps of the "thing poems" in *New Poems*. In a letter to a reader inquiring about a sonnet's symbolism, Rilke wrote: "You are thinking too far out beyond the poem itself . . . I believe that no poem in the *Sonnets to Orpheus* means anything that is not fully written out there, often it is true, with its most secret name. All (external) allusion would be contradictory to the indescribably 'being there' of the poem."

The sequence, of course, begins with the odd image of Orpheus as a "tree" springing up in the ear. A visual image of no particular emotional weight except maybe that of a painful growth. But it melodically glides to sonority, bursting its seed into fertility with Orpheus's "tree" becoming an enchanted natural cathedral where the forest animals can come to be blessed.

> . . . a temple of resonance
> in their deepest hearing, a refuge of darkest desire,
> an entrance of trembling door posts.

In the Orpheus sonnets, Rilke works at the seams and the edges—the sun-flecked places in clouds where rain appears. Translating them, you're aware of a sense of the not quite there, images as ephemeral as smoke signals, and the uneasy feeling that reality is just one face of things. An elusive sense that on the indivisible continuum of time, even as we live, we're already dead.

The sequence meanders and digresses, but again and again returns to twin themes of music and death. Rilke dedicated the Orpheus sonnets to Vera Knoop, a former playmate of his daughter, a talented dancer and old family friend who died of leukemia on the cusp of becoming an adult. Only the penultimate sonnets of each part explicitly speak to Vera. But her presence seems implicit not only in the "Spanish Dancer" reminiscent imagery of Sonnet 2, XVIII, but also in the quiet maiden of the 2, IV "Unicorn" Sonnet, and in the "girlish fingers" of the "weeping water nymph" Grief in Sonnet I, VIII."

Some have interpreted Part One, II's "almost a girl" as referring to Vera. I tend to read it as also relating to Rilke's strange own early life, when his mother dressed him as a girl and called him "Renee" until he was old enough to go to school. But even that evocation of his own lost girlhood can be said to reach out in sorority with the lost Vera.

Some four years later, Rilke himself died of leukemia at the relatively young age of fifty-two. The disease was undiagnosed and presumably had not yet even presented at the time of the Sonnets' composition. But it's hard, translating these poems, not to infer a sense of unconscious prescience, of signals from the disease still latent, but beginning to stir in his blood.

In that sense the Sonnets to Orpheus are not only rich with death, but imbued with Rilke's own demise, still unaware of that weight about to fall. For Rilke in the Sonnets, death and the dead seem like deep bass notes from an organ preparing to soar. At least so he hoped? Not the rumbling of a pitiless volcano . . . but the Minotaur's cold curious breath.

I

Da stieg ein Baum. O reine Übersteigüng!
O Orpheus singt! O hoher Baum im Ohr!
Und alles schwieg. Doch selbst in der Verschweigung
ging neuer Anfang, Wink und Wandlung vor.

Tiere aus Stille drangen aus dem klaren
gelösten Wald von Lager und Genist;
und da ergab sich, daß sie nicht aus List
und nicht aus Angst in sich so leise waren,

sondern aus Hören. Brüllen, Schrei, Geröhr
schien klein in ihren Herzen. Und wo eben
kaum eine Hütte war, dies zu empfangen,

ein Unterschlupf aus dunkelstem Verlangen
mit einem Zugang, dessen Pfosten beben,—
da schufst du ihnen Tempel im Gehör.

I

In the attentive stillness, there climbed a tree . . .
O utter overabundance. O Orpheus silent and singing.
O tall tree rooted in the ear. And everything still to be
said. This is how something new quietly approaches, winks,

then begins to transform. Just as once—from their lairs
and nests—from the freed, untangling forest—the animals trooped
in their silence: As it's told, neither cunning nor fear
made them so gentle, so self contained.

They were simply listening. Their shrieks, moos
and roars shriveled to something tiny in the corners
of their hearts. And where barely even a shed once stood

to receive them—you created a temple of resonance
in their deepest hearing, a refuge of darkest desire,
an entrance of trembling door posts.

II

Und fast ein Mädchen wars und ging hervor
aus diesem einigen Glück von Sang und Leier
und glänzte klar durch ihre Frühlingsschleier
und machte sich ein Bett in meinem Ohr.

Und schlief in mir. Und alles war ihr Schlaf.
Die Bäume, die ich je bewundert, diese
fühlbare Ferne, die gefühlte Wiese
und jedes Staunen, das mich selbst betraf.

Sie schlief die Welt. Singender Gott, wie hast
du sie vollendet, daß sie nicht begehrte,
erst wach zu sein? Sieh, sie erstand und schlief.

Wo ist ihr Tod? O, wirst du dies Motiv
erfinden noch, eh sich dein Lied verzehrte?—
Wo sinkt sie hin aus mir?... Ein Mädchen fast...

II

Well, *it nearly was a girl:* She arose
out of that inseparable joy of song and lyre.
And shimmering clearly through her springtime haze
she made a bed for herself in my ear.

And slept in me. But everything was in that sleep.
The wonder in the trees, those tangible
beckoning distances, the meadows underfoot
and every astonishment that seized me.

She slept the world. Singing god, how were
you able to perfect her without her demanding to be
the one who awoke? Look, how she walked in her sleep.

Where is her death? Ah, will you be able to explore
this motif before your song runs out? Where
is she ebbing from me? . . . *A girl, nearly* . . .

III

Ein Gott vermags. Wie aber, sag mir, soll
Mann ihm folgen durch die schmale Leier?
Sinn ist Zwiespalts. An der Kreuzung zweier
Herzwege steht kein Tempel für Apoll.

Gesang, wie du ihn lehrst, ist nicht Begehr,
nicht Werbung um ein endlich noch Erreichtes;
Gesang ist Dasein. Für den Gott ein Leichtes.
Wann aber *sind* wir? Und wann wendet er

an unser Sein die Erde und die Sterne?
Dies ists nicht, Jüngling, daß du liebst, wenn auch
die Stimme dann den Mund dir aufstößt,—lerne

vergessen, daß du aufsangst. Das verrinnt.
In Wahrheit singen, ist ein andrer Hauch.
Ein Hauch um nichts. Ein Wehn im Gott. Ein Wind.

III

A god's empowered. But tell me how any human is
supposed to follow him through that narrow lyre.
Our minds are always divided. There aren't any temples
to Apollo at the crossroads of the ambivalent heart.

Singing, as you teach it, isn't longing. Isn't
campaigning for something you finally attain.
Song is being. Easy for divinity,
but when do we—simply exist? And when

are we handed the earth and the stars as a gift?
That's not it, child; even if you're in love, so breathless
your helpless voice simply bursts from your mouth.

Remember to forget your spontaneous songs. They'll
run their course. Real singing requires another breath.
A breath of nothing, a riffle in God, a wind.

IV

O ihr Zärtlichen, tretet zuweilen
in den Atem, der euch nicht meint,
laßt ihn an eueren Wangen sich teilen,
hinter euch zittert er, wieder vereint.

O ihr Seligen, o ihr Heilen,
die ihr der Anfang der Herzen scheint
Bogen der Pfeile und Ziele von Pfeilen,
ewiger glänzt euer Lächeln verweint.

Fürchtet euch nicht zu leiden, die Schwere,
gebt sie zurück an der Erde Gewicht;
schwer sind die Berge, schwer sind die Meere.

Selbst die als Kinder ihr pflanztet, die Bäume,
wurden zu schwer längst; ihr trüget sie nicht.
Aber die Lüfte ... aber die Räume....

IV

Ah, you beloved dears: step out once
in a while into a breath that pays you no
mind. Let it part itself on your cheeks, then
shiver behind you as it reunites again.

Ah you blessed, you all of one piece,
you who always seem so fresh of heart.
Bows for your arrows and targets for arrows,
your smiles always bright through the tears.

Don't be so afraid of trouble, of what's
serious. You owe it to the heavy earth,
the brooding mountains, the serious ocean.

The saplings you, yourselves, planted as children
have long ago grown too heavy for you to bear.
But the breeze . . . those wide open spaces.

V

Errichtet keinen Denkstein. Laßt die Rose
nur jedes Jahr zu seinen Gunsten blühn.
Denn Orpheus ists. Seine Metamorphose
in dem und dem. Wir sollen uns nicht mühn

um andre Namen. Ein für alle Male
ists Orpheus, wenn es singt. Er kommt und geht.
Ists nicht schon viel, wem, er die Rosenschale
um ein paar Tage manchmal übersteht?

O wie er schwinden muß, daß ihrs begrifft!
Und wenn ihm selbst auch bangte, daß er schwände.
Indem sein Wort das Hiersein übertrifft,

ist er schon dort, wohin ihrs nicht begleitet.
Der Leier Gitter zwängt ihm nicht die Hände.
Und er gehorcht, indem er überschreitet.

V

Don't erect his monuments in stone. Just let
the rose bloom each spring as his token. Because
roses are Orpheus too—just another of his metamorphoses
into one thing or another. Why torture ourselves

deciphering all his names? Everything that sings—
now and forever—is Orpheus as he comes and goes.
So isn't it enough if every so often he lingers
a few days with the rose petals in the bowl?

So much of him has to wither so you can know.
It frightens him too, as he fades. But just as his
word transcends what's here, what's now—

he's already there, alone where you can't be.
The bars of the lyre strings don't cramp his
fingers. Even transgressing, he obeys.

VI

Ist er ein Hiesiger? Nein, aus beiden
Reichen erwuchs seine weite Natur.
Kundiger böge die Zweige der Weiden,
wer die Wurzeln der Weiden erfuhr.

Geht ihr zu Bette, so laßt auf dem Tische
Brot nicht und Milch nicht; die Toten ziehtes—.
Aber er, der Beschwörende, mische
unter der Milde des Augenlids

ihre Erscheinung in alles Geschaute;
und der Zauber von Erdrauch und Raute
sei ihm so wahr wie der klarste Bezug.

Nichts kann das gültige Bild ihm verschlimmern;
sei es aus Gräbern, sei es aus Zimmern,
rühme er Fingerring, Spange und Krug.

VI

Is he someone from here—just one of us? No,
both realms nurtured that expansive heart.
He learned how to bend the weeping willow
branch from the willow's own sad roots.

At night, when you go to bed, never leave bread,
never leave milk on the table. It draws the dead.
But under the caress of sleeping
eyelids, he—the initiate—will mingle their

intimate tokens into everything you dream.
To him, the magic summons of burnt earth-smoke
and rue is a transparent logic. Nothing

can decay his images: not the grave, not
the living in their rooms, as he infuses
finger ring, hair clasp and jug with his praise.

VII

Rühmen, das ists! Ein zum Rühmen Bestellter,
ging er hervor wie das Erz aas des Steins
Schweigen. Sein Herz, o vergängliche Kelter
eines den Menschen unendlichen Weins.

Nie versagt ihm die Stimme am Staube,
wenn ihn das göttliche Beispiel ergreift.
Alles wird Weinberg, alles wird Traube,
in seinem fühlenden Süden gereift.

Nicht in den Grüften der Könige Moder
straft ihm die Rühmung Lügen, oder
daß von den Göttern ein Schatten fällt.

Er ist einer der bleibenden Boten,
der noch weit in die Türen der Toten
Schalen mit rühmlichen Früchten hält.

VII

That's what it's all about: Praise and all its glory.
From one who's on a mission of praise, glittering
like ore in the mute stone. His humanity
a mortal grape press, squeezing out eternal wine.

Because even choked with dust his voice never
forsakes him when divinity seizes. Everything
becomes vineyard, everything ripens
like grapes clustered in the rich southern sun.

Neither the mold that claims the graves
of kings, nor the shadow that falls
from the gods, makes a lie of his praise.

He's one of the enduring messengers. A friend,
who deep within the portals of the dead, still
offers the glorious fruit and the brimming bowl.

VIII

Nur im Raum der Rühmung darf die Klage
gehn, die Nymphe des geweinten Quells,
wachend über unserm Niederschlage,
daß er klar sei an demselben Fels,

der die Tore trägt und die Altäre.—
Sieh, um Ihre stillen Schultern früht
das Gefühl, daß sie die jüngste wäre
unter den Geschwistern im Gemüt.

Jubel *weiß*, und Sehnsucht ist geständig,—
nur die Klage lernt noch; mädchenhändig
zählt sie nächtelang das alte Schlimme.

Aber plötzlich, schräg und ungeübt,
hält sie doch ein Sternbild unsrer Stimme
in den Himmel, den ihr Hauch nicht trübt.

VIII

Grief—that water nymph of the weeping
fountain is only allowed to wander the places we
value. So isn't it obvious that our depression—
which she tends—springs from the same

rock we quarry for our doorways and altars?
Look how her quiet, vulnerable shoulders
betray she's the youngest among
the sisters who grace our moods.

Jubilation *knows*, and Longing's already confessed.
Only Grief's still learning her role.
All night long she enumerates the ancient wrongs

on girlish fingers. Yet suddenly, surprised
and raw, a constellation of our voices leaps
out of her into the sky untouched by her breath.

IX

Nur wer die Leier schon hob
auch unter Schatten,
darf das unendliche Lob
ahnend erstatten.

Nur wer mit Toten vom Mohn
aß, von dem ihren,
wird nicht den leisesten Ton
wieder verlieren.

Mag auch die Spieglung im Teich
oft uns verschwimmen:
Wisse das Bild.

Erst in dem Doppelbereich
werden die Stimmen
ewig und mild.

IX

Only someone who's
lifted the lyre among shadows
as well—is allowed to return
eternal praise to the divine.

Only someone who's
eaten poppies with the dead—
will be sure to never lose
that subtle harmony again.

It may even be a mirage
swimming in the pool,
but take in that image.

Only in the dual
kingdom can eternal
music mellow and endure.

X

Euch, die ihr nie mein Gefühl verließt,
grüß ich, antikische Sarkophage,
die das fröhliche Wasser römischer Tage
als ein wandelndes Lied durchfließt.

Oder jene so offenen, wie das Aug
eines frohen erwachenden Hirten,
—innen voll Stille und Bienensaug—
denen entzückte Falter entschwirrten;

alle, die man dem Zweifel entreißt,
grüß ich, die wiedergeöffneten Munde,
die schon wußten, was schweigen heißt.

Wissen wirs, Freunde, wissen wirs nicht?
Beides bildet die zögernde Stunde
in dem menschlichen Angesicht.

X

You, for whom I've never lost my
feelings, I greet you, ancient sarcophagi,
through whom the same glad water of Roman
days flows like a running song. Or one

of those others, vacated in the graveyard—
as wide open as the eye of a shepherd
awakening to joy—flitting with charmed
butterflies—full of quiet and honey inside.

I greet those gaping re-opened mouths
torn away from any doubts,
who know now, what silence means.

We know, friends—or we really
don't? The choice becomes
a hesitant lesson in the human face.

XI

Sieh den Himmel. Heißt kein Sternbild "Reiter"?
Denn dies ist uns seltsam eingeprägt:
dieser Stolz aus Erde. Und ein zweiter,
der ihn treibt und hält und den er trägt.

Ist nicht so, gejagt und dann gebändigt,
diese sehnige Natur des Seins?
Weg und Wendung. Doch ein Druck verständigt.
Neue Weite. Und die zwei sind eins.

Aber *sind* sie's? Oder meinen beide
nicht den Weg, den sie zusammen tun?
Namenlos schon trennt sie Tisch und Weide.

Auch die sternische Verbindung trügt,
Doch uns freue eine Weile nun,
der Figur zu glauben. Das genügt.

XI

Look, there in the sky. If there isn't a constellation
named "Rider", there should be. Because the thing's so
ingrained in us: That pride of the earth. And another—
who spurs, then halts it—and who it bears.

Isn't this just how we urge on, then
rein in our own sinewy natures? Straight
ahead—a turn—just a touch conveys.
New distances. The two as if they were one

But are they? Or does each travel the same
path for their own quiet reasons—
separated utterly by table and pasture.

Because even the patterns of stars are illusion.
Let's just be happy to be here awhile. It's
enough to pretend there's connection.

XII

Heil dem Geist, der uns verbinden mag;
denn wir leben wahrhaft in Figuren.
Und mit kleinen Schritten gehn die Uhren
neben unserm eigentlichen Tag.

Ohne unsern wahren Platz zu kennen,
handeln wir aus wirklichem Bezug.
Die Antennen fühlen die Antennen,
und die leere Ferne trug....

Reine Spannung. O Musik der Kräfte!
Ist nicht durch die läßlichen Geschäfte
jede Störung von dir abgelenkt?

Selbst wenn sich der Bauer sorgt und handelt,
wo die Saat in Sommer sich verwandelt,
reicht er niemals hin. Die Erde *schenkt*.

XII

Hail to the spirit that's able to connect
us. Because we really do spring to life
in patterns. The way clocks map out our practical
day in precise little steps.

Never sure of where we actually stand, we
still pursue what's workable.
Antennae sense antennae,
and the open spaces yield . . .

Pure electricity—the raw music of power!
Isn't it our self indulgent exploitation
that strips the static from you?

But as much as the farmer calculates and worries
he can never reach down where the seed
becomes summer, and the earth *provides.*

XIII

Voller Apfel, Birne und Banane,
Stachelbeere ... Alles dieses spricht
Tod und Leben in den Mund ... Ich ahne ...
Lest es einem Kind vom Angesicht,

wenn es sie erschmeckt. Dies kommt von weit.
Wird euch langsam namenlos im Munde?
Wo sonst Worte waren, fließen Funde,
aus dem Fruchtfleisch überrascht befreit.

Wagt zu sagen, was ihr Apfel nennt.
Diese Süße, die sich erst verdichtet,
um, im Schmecken leise aufgerichtet,

klar zu werden, wach und transparent,
doppeldeutig, sonnig, erdig, hiesig—:
O Erfahrung, Fühlung, Freude—, riesig!

XIII

Ripe apple, pear and banana.
Gooseberry. They all speak death and life
to the mouth. I suspect, can
read it in a child's smile

as he tastes them: This comes from a long
way off. A nameless language, slowly
forming on the tongue. In place of words, discoveries
set free from the surprised fruit-meat.

Go ahead, try. Define the thing we call Apple.
The sweetness, rich and dense at first,
then gently rising until the taste

becomes clarified, awake, transparent:
The double taste of sun and earth.
Living, feeling, happy—immense.

XIV

Wir gehen um mit Blume, Weinblatt, Frucht.
Sie sprechen nicht die Sprache nur des Jahres.
Aus Dunkel steigt ein buntes Offenbares
und hat vielleicht den Glanz der Eifersucht

der Toten an sich, die die Erde stärken.
Was wissen wir von ihrem Teil an dem?
Es ist seit lange ihre Art, den Lehm
mit ihnem freien Marke zu durchmärken.

Nun fragt sich nur: tun sie es gern?...
Drängt diese Frucht, ein Werk von schweren Sklaven,
geballt zu uns empor, zu ihren Herrn?

Sind sie die Herrn, die bei den Wurzeln schlafen,
und gönnen uns aus ihren Überflüssen
dies Zwischending aus stummer Kraft und Küssen?

XIV

We're companions to the flower, the vine leaf,
the fruit. They don't just speak the changing language
of the seasons. But a multicolored revelation that climbs
from darkness with a glint, perhaps, of the envy

of the dead who loam and fortify the earth.
How can we ever guess their share
in this? It's their ancient nature to mingle
and marry their liberated marrow with the clay.

So you have to ask yourself: Is this something
they want to do? Is it the work of laboring slaves—
the fruit forced up like a clenched fist to us, their masters

above? Or are they the masters? The ones who sleep
in the roots and grant us out of their abundance
this hybrid of speechless strength and kisses.

XV

Wartet..., das schmeckt ... Schon ists auf der Flucht.
... Wenig Musik nur, ein Stampfen, ein Summen—:
Mädchen, ihr warmen, Mädchen, ihr stummen,
tanzt den Geschmack der erfahrenen Frucht!

Tanzt die Orange. Wer kann sie vergessen,
wie sie, ertrinkend in sich, sich wehrt
wider ihr Süßsein. Ihr habt sie besessen.
Sie hat sich köstlich zu euch bekehrt.

Tanzt die Orange. Die wärmere Landschaft,
werft sie aus euch, daß die reife erstrahle
in Lüften der Heimat! Erglühte, enthüllt

Düfte um Düfte! Schafft die Verwandtschaft
mit der reinen, sich weigernden Schale,
mit dem Saft, der die glückliche füllt!

XV

Wait... that's tasty...already, it's taking flight.
. . . Just a little music, a foot tap, a hum—
You girls, so affectionate and so mum,
 can you dance the savor that lives in the just eaten fruit?

Dance the orange that you can't forget:
The way, drowning in its juice,
it struggles against its very own sweetness.
The way you obsessed
and possessed it.

Dance the orange: The warm country.
Exude it, let it ripen and radiate like a breeze
in the house. Let yourselves glow and unveil

your fragrance, scent after scent. Mend
the relationship between the chaste, self
denying peel and the juice that fills it with joy.

XVI

Du, mein Freund, bist einsam, weil ...
Wir machen mit Worten und Fingerzeigen
uns allmählich die Welt zu eigen,
vielleicht ihren schwächsten, gefährlichsten Teil.

Wer zeigt mit Fingern auf einen Geruch?—
Doch von den Kräften, die uns bedrohten,
fühlst du viele ... Du kennst die Toten,
und du erschrickst vor dem Zauberspruch.

Sieh, nun heißt es zusammen ertragen
Stückwerk und Teile, als sei es das Ganze.
Dir helfen, wird schwer sein. Vor allem: pflanze

mich nicht in dein Herz. Ich wüchse zu schnell.
Doch *meines* Herrn Hand will ich führen und sagen:
Hier. Das ist Esau in seinem Fell.

XVI

You, my shaggy friend, are lonely. Because . . . ?
We humans create a world for ourselves,
gradually, with words and clues. A territory
of our own, perhaps the weakest, most precarious

portion. None of us have clues to what you smell.
You sense so many more of the forces
that menace us . . . You recognize the dead,
and slink in fright from magic spells.

Can you see now how we have to bear the task
together, of perceiving piecework and parts as a whole?
Helping you is going to be hard. Whatever you do:

Don't plant me in your heart. I grow too fast.
But I will take *my master* Orpheus' hand, and tell
him: Here, This is Esau in his pelt.

XVII

Zu unterst der Atte, verworrn,
all der Erbauten
Wurzel, verborgener Born,
den sie nie schauten.

Sturmhelm und Jägerhorn,
Spruch von Ergrauten,
Männer im Bruderzorn,
Frauen wie Lauten....

Drängender Zweig an Zweig,
nirgends ein freier...
Einer! o stei g... o steig....

Aber sie brechen noch.
Dieser erst oben doch
biegt sich zur Leier.

XVII

Ingrown under the willow—
the old one—the root
of everything we inherit,
the secret spring no one ever saw.

Hunting horns and battle helmets.
The edicts of the elders.
Brother against brother.
Women like lutes...

Branch crowding out branch.
Nowhere to break free...
Then one! Climb, oh climb . . .

The rest will all break.
Only the topmost branch
can be bent into a lyre.

XVIII

Hörst du das Neue, Herr,
dröhnen und beben?
Kommen Verkündiger,
die es erheben.

Zwar ist kein Hören heil
in dem Durchtobtsein,
doch der Maschinenteil
will jetzt gelobt sein.

Sieh, die Maschine:
wie sie sich wälzt und rächt
und uns entstellt und schwächt.

Hat sie aus uns auch Kraft,
sie, ohne Leidenschaft,
treibe und diene.

XVIII

Master: Can you hear modernity
booming and shaking?
Its prophets and proponents
busily singing its praises?

The message comes in fits and
starts in a thoroughgoing frenzy.
But it's clear what the mechanizers want :
nothing less—our whole hearted loyalty.

Look at the machines: how
they roll and avenge, belittle
and mutilate. Yet their power

derives from—is strictly—
our own invention. These
driven passionless servants.

XIX

Wandelt sich rasch auch die Welt
wie Wolkengestalten,
alles Vollendete fällt
heim zum Uralten.

Über dem Wandel und Gang,
weiter und freier,
währt noch dein Vor-Gesang,
Gott mit der Leier.

Nicht sind die Leiden erkannt,
nicht ist die Liebe gelernt,
und was im Tod uns entfernt,

ist nicht entschleiert.
Einzig das Lied überm land
heiligt und feiert.

XIX

Our world transforms itself
as quickly as cloud formations shift.
Once a pattern's fulfilled, it
falls like rain coming home to the oldest

roots. Above the changing paths,
larger and free to go where
you please; your music resonates
and guides—god with the lyre.

Suffering is never explained.
Love is undefinable. And
what takes us away when we die

can't be ever revealed. But your
song remains the consoling ceremony
that consecrates the air.

XX

Dir aber, Herr, o was weih ich dir, sag,
der das Ohr den Geschöpfen gelehrt?—
Mein Erinnern an einen Frühlingstag,
seinen Abend, in Rußland—, ein Pferd....

Herüber vom Dorf kam der Schimmel allein,
an der vorderen Fessel den Pflock,
um die Nacht auf den Wiesen allein zu sein;
wie schlug seiner Mähne Gelock

an den Hals im Takte des Übermuts,
bei dem grob gehemmten Galopp.
Wie sprangen die Quellen des Rossebluts!

Der fühlte die Weiten, und ob!
der sang und der hörte—, dein Sagenkreis
war in ihm geschlossen.
Sein Bild: ich weih's.

XX

But is there anything I could consecrate
to you—the Master who teaches all creatures
what it means to hear? My memory of a spring day,
its evening actually, in Russia—a horse...

From a village off some way, the white
horse came, dragging a fetter and stake
from his foreleg. His curled mane
wild to be alone on the meadow at night.

His neck twisting to follow the dance of that
crudely hampered gallop in time with
the pumping fountain of his stallion's heart.

He sensed the open spaces and every bit
of him sang—and listened. Your myths
came full circle in him.
I offer: his image.

XXI

Frühling ist wiedergekommen. Die Erde
ist wie ein Kind, das Gedichte weiß;
viele, o viele ... Für die Beschwerde
langen Lernens bekommt sie den Preis.

Streng war ihr Lehrer. Wir mochten das Weiße
an dem Barte des alten Manns.
Nun, wie du Grüne, das Blaue heiße,
dürfen wir fragen: sie kanns, sie kanns!

Erde, die frei hat, du glückliche, spiele
nun mit den Kindern. Wir wollen dich fangen,
fröhliche Erde. Dem Frohsten gelingt.

O, was der Lehrer sie lehrte, das Viele,
und was gedruckt steht in Wurzeln und langen
schwierigen Stämmen: sie singts, sie singts!

XXI

Spring's returned again. The earth is like a child;
forced to memorize too many verses, over
and over; who's painfully learned her
tedious lessons so well—She's won the prize.

Who wouldn't love all the white in that old man's beard?
But her teacher was so strict with her. Now
it's green we're curious about, and just what there
is that intrigues us with blue. She knows all the answers.

Lucky earth is on vacation, playing
with the kids. We're chasing you, we'll
catch you silly earth. Whoever's happiest wins.

The exercises that unrelenting disciplinarian
imposed: The recitation of roots, patience
with the tendril's struggle—are finally bursting into song.

XXII

Wir sind die Treibenden.
Aber den Schritt der Zeit,
nehmt ihn als Kleinigkeit
im immer Bleibenden.

Alles das Eilende
wird schon vorüber sein;
denn das Verweilende
erst weiht uns ein.

Knaben, o werft den Mut
nicht in die Schnelligkeit,
nicht in den Flugversuch.

Alles ist ausgeruht:
Dunkel und Helligkeit,
Blume und Buch.

XXII

We're always so
driven. But the pace
of time is a trivial detail
in the eternal now.

Everything hurrying to become
has already come to pass.
Because the destination
is what draws us.

Boys, don't waste your courage
on speed, on the conquest
of the air.

Everything's already at rest.
Darkness and brilliance,
word and flower.

XXIII

O erst dann, wenn der Flug
nicht mehr um seinetwillen
wird in die Himmelstillen
steigen, sich selber genug,

um in lichten Profilen,
als das Gerät, das gelang,
Liebling der Winde zu spielen,
sicher schwenkend und schlank,—

erst wenn ein reines Wohin
wachsender Apparate
Knabenstolz überwiegt,

wird, überstürzt von Gewinn,
jener den Fernen Genahte
sein, was er einsam erfliegt.

XXIII

Only then: After flight's
no longer what we
do just for the sake of flying.
When we're able to rest in the silent

blue. When that glittering profile
in the sun, the slim darling and
plaything of the winds has
become just another successful

tool—will pure utility
outweigh our childish pride. Only
then will we claim the dizzy

prize of destination,
of distance erased by proximity,
a sky we finally own.

XXIV

Sollen wir unsere uralte Freundschaft, die großen
niemals werbenden Götter, weil sie der harte
Stahl, den wir streng erzogen, nicht kennt, verstoßen
oder sie plötzlich suchen auf einer Karte?

Diese gewaltigen Freunde, die uns die Toten
nehmen, rühren nirgends an unsere Räder.
Unsere Gastmähler haben wir weit—, unsere Bäder,
fortgerückt, und ihre uns lang schon zu langsamen Boten

überholen wir immer. Einsamer nun auf einander
ganz angewiesen, ohne einander zu kennen,
führen wir nicht mehr die Pfade als schöne Mäander,

sondern als Grade. Nur noch in Dampfkesseln brennen
die einstigen Feuer und heben die Hämmer, die immer
größern. Wir aber nehmen an Kraft ab, wie Schwimmer.

XXIV

Should we end our age-old fellowship with the great gods—who
never did advertise their presence—just because the hard steel
we've so austerely tempered can't recognize them? Or should we
scramble to find them somewhere on our charts? Those

violent allies who spirit the dead from us without touching
our machinery anywhere. We've civilized our feasts, dismantled
the public baths—and for such a long time now their
    messengers have
been too slow: We outrun them every time. The loneliness
    of being

totally dependent just on each other—and unable to
    understand
each other. We never mark out those beautiful meandering
trails anymore. We've learned to grade our roads in
    straight lines.

It's only in the boiler room that we burn with the original fire,
the pistons pounding themselves into something always larger.
While our power continues to fail us, like swimmers.

XXV

Dich aber will ich nun, dich, die ich kannte
wie eine Blume, von der ich den Namen nicht weiß,
noch ein Mal erinnern und ihnen zeigen, Entwandte,
schöne Gespielin des unüberwindlichen Schrei's.

Tänzerin erst, die plötzlich, den Körper voll Zögern,
anhielt, als göß man ihr Jungsein in Erz;
trauernd und lauschend—. Da, von den hohen Vermögern,
fiel ihr Musik in das veränderte Herz.

Nah war die Krankheit. Schon von den Schatten bemächtigt,
drängte verdunkelt das Blut, doch, wie flüchtig verdächtigt,
trieb es in seinen natürlichen Frühling hervor.

Wieder und wieder, von Dunkel und Stürz unterbrochen,
glänzte es irdisch. Bis es nach schrecklichem Pochen
trat in das trostlos offene Tor.

XXV

Only now, finally, can I try to honor your memory.
You who I knew like a flower when I barely
knew your name. Lost, beautiful
playmate of the unquenchable yell.

You began to dance, but suddenly your body—overcome
with hesitation—paused. As if your very youth
were being cast in bronze. Then from the powers
on high, a music fell that altered your heart.

The illness was imminent. Already seized by shadows, your
blood was pulsing darkness. But it was still just a fleeting
    suspicion:
the expectable uncertain pulse of your April years?

Again and again the intervals of darkness and ruin returned
Your blood slickened with earth and pounded like a hammer.
The door hopelessly opened—and you entered.

XXVI

Du aber, Göttlicher, du, bis zuletzt noch Ertöner,
da ihn der Schwarm der verschmähten Mänaden befiel,
hast ihr Geschrei übertönt mit Ordnung, du Schöner,
aus den Zerstörenden stieg dein erbauendes Spiel.

Keine war da, daß sie Haupt dir und Leier zerstör',
wie sie auch rangen und rasten; und alle die scharfen
Steine, die sie nach deinem Herzen warfen,
wurden zu Sanftem an dir und begabt mit Gehör.

Schließlich zerschlugen sie dich, von der Rache gehetzt,
während dein Klang noch in Löwen und Felsen verweilte
und in den Bäumen und Vögeln. Dort singst du noch jetzt.

O du verlorener Gott! Du unendliche Spur!
Nur weil dich reißend zuletzt die Feindschaft verteilte,
sind wir die Hörenden jetzt und ein Mund der Natur.

XXVI

But you, the demigod, still intoned until the end.
When the swarm of scorned Maenads brought you down,
you harmonized their shrieks. Out of that mayhem
your grand performance soared.

None of them—in all their wresting rage—
could hurt your head or your lyre. The jagged
stones they jabbed at your heart softened
as they touched you, then grew ears.

Eventually they tore you to pieces. They
had their vengeance—but your resonance
lingered in the rocks among lions, birds and trees.

Forsaken god. Eternal echo and scent. Only
because of the hate that rent and scattered you
does nature have a voice that speaks with us.

I

Atmen, du unsichtbares Gedicht!
Immerfort um das eigne
Sein rein eingetauschter Weltraum. Gegengewicht,
in dem ich mich rhythmisch ereigne.

Einzige Welle, deren
allmähliches Meer ich bin;
sparsamstes du von allen möglichen Meeren,—
Raumgewinn.

Wie viele von diesen Stellen der Räume waren schon
innen in mir. Manche Winde
sind wie mein Sohn.

Erkennst du mich, Luft, du, voll noch einst meiniger Orte?
Du, einmal glatte Rinde,
Rundung und Blatt meiner Worte.

I

Breath, you imperceptible poem!
Constantly pulling our splintered existence
into genuine commerce with the universe.
Counterpoint whose dance I rhythmically become.

Unique wave, in which
I gradually become a sea,
the most frugal of possible
seas—hoarding new spaces.

How much crowded space has already
passed through me? Many a wind seems
like a son. Air, do you recognize me? You're

still full of places that once were
mine, still rich with the polished birch
and curve and leaf of my old words.

II

So wie dem Meister manchmal das eilig
nähere Blatt den *wirklichen* Strich
abnimmt: so nehmen oft Spiegel das heilig
einzige Lächeln der Mädchen in sich,

wenn sie den Morgen erproben, allein,—
oder im Glanze der dienenden Lichter.
Und in das Atmen der echten Gesichter,
später, fällt nur ein Widerschein,

Was haben Augen einst ins umrußte
lange Verglühn der Kamine geschaut:
Blicke des Lebens, für immer verlorne.

Ach, der Erde, wer kennt die Verluste?
Nur, wer mit dennoch preisendem Laut
sänge das Herz, das ins Ganze geborne.

II

The way, sometimes, the master's most
authentic line is hastily captured in whatever
sketchbook comes to hand—that's the way a mirror
might idly steal a young woman's sacred, most

private smile—as she tests the morning, alone—
or in the glow of flattering candles.
Then the breath in her real face
fades to just a reflection. What happens

to eyes that stare for hours
as the fireplace flickers from ember
to coal—locked in a gaze with life lost forever?

Who knows how much we constantly lose
on this earth? Only someone who despite it all
still sings the praises of the heart born whole.

III

Spiegel: noch nie hat man wissend beschrieben,
was ihr in euerem Wesen seid.
Ihr, wie mit lauter Löchern von Sieben
erfüllten Zwischenräume der Zeit.

Ihr, noch des leeren Saales Verschwender—,
wenn es dämmert, wie Wälder weit....
Und der Lüster geht wie ein Sechzehn-Ender
durch eure Unbetretbarkeit.

Manchmal seid ihr voll Malerei.
Einige scheinen in euch gegangen—,
andere schicktet ihr scheu vorbei.

Aber die Schönste wird bleiben, bis
drüben in ihre enthaltenen Wangen
eindrang der klare gelöste Narziß.

III

Mirrors—no one has ever been able to really guess
who you are when you're alone with yourselves:
When the spaces between time sift
like water through your sieve.

You profligates of the empty room—
as deep as the woods at dusk where
candlelight wanders like an antlered
stag trapped behind your impenetrable glow.

Some of your rooms are rich with portraits
and a few are allowed to enter, deep inside.
Others you shyly avoid.

But someday the fairest of them all will arrive and linger,
and deny herself to you—until you set Narcissus free
to brighten her haughty cheeks.

IV

O dieses ist das Tier, das es nicht gibt.
Sie wußtens nicht und habens jeden Falls
—sein Wandeln, seine Haltung, seinen Hals,
bis in des stillen Blickes Licht—geliebt.

Zwar war es nicht. Doch weil sie's liebten, ward
ein reines Tier. Sie ließen immer Raum.
Und in dem Raume, klar und ausgespart,
erhob es leicht sein Haupt und brauchte kaum

zu sein. Sie nährten es mit keinem Korn,
nur immer mit der Möglichkeit, es sei.
Und die gab solche Stärke an das Tier,

daß es aus sich ein Stirnhorn trieb. Ein Horn.
Zu einer Jungfrau kam es weiß herbei—
und war im Silber-Spiegel und in ihr.

IV

O, this is the animal that could never be.
They searched and couldn't find it, but even so:
It's walk, it's poise, the set of its neck, the quiet
light in its eyes—they were enthralled with it.

It never was. But because they loved it,
it became the purest animal. They were always
careful to leave space for it. And in that clearing
unmolested and apart, it lifted its head so easily

it hardly had to bother to be. They never fed
it grain, only the eternal possibility it might occur.
And this gave so much strength to the creature

that it grew a horn from its forehead. A single
horn. Came up softly in its white coat behind a virgin
and existed in her silver mirror and in herself.

V

Blumenmuskel, der der Anemone
Wiesenmorgen nach und nach erschließt,
bis in ihren Schoß das polyphone
Licht der lauten Himmel sich ergießt,

in den stillen Blütenstern gespannter
Muskel des unendlichen Empfangs,
manchmal *so* von Fülle übermannter,
daß der Ruhewink des Untergangs

kaum vermag die weitzurückgeschnellten
Blätterränder dir zurückzugeben:
du, Entschluß und Kraft von *wieviel* Welten!

Wir Gewaltsmen, wir währen länger.
Aber *wann*, in welchem aller Leben,
sind wir endlich offen und Empfänger?

V

Flower-muscle: The way you, ever so
slowly, open the anemone to the meadow
morning, until the polyphonic light
of the singing sky pours into your womb.

Infinitely receptive muscle. Tensed
by your quiet star-blossom. Sometimes *so*
overpowered by fullness, that the sleepy
nods of the dying sun can barely bequeath

your contorted wide open petals
back to yourself. You—the goal
and energy of *how many* worlds.

We movers and tramplers live longer.
But *when*, in which one of all those lives,
will we finally be open enough to receive?

VI

Rose, du thronende, denen im Altertume
warst du ein Kelch mit einfachem Rand.
Uns aber bist du die volle zahllose Blume,
der unerschöpfliche Gegenstand.

In deinem Reichtum scheinst du wie Kleidung um Kleidung
um einen Leib aus nichts als Glanz;
aber dein einzelnes Blatt ist zugleich die Vermeidung
und die Verleugnung jedes Gewands.

Seit Jahrhunderten ruft uns dein Duft
seine süßesten Namen herüber;
plötzlich liegt er wie Ruhm in der Luft.

Dennoch, wir wisssen ihn nicht zu nennen, wir raten•
Und Erinnerung geht zu ihm über,
die wir von rufbaren Stunden erbaten.

VI

Enthroned rose: In the old days
you were a chalice with a simple brim.
But, now—you've fully bloomed *for us*,
an infinitely, inexhaustible subject.

In your richness you're like cloak upon
cloak covering a body of nothing but
light. All the while each individual petal
eludes and disdains all costumes.

For centuries your perfume and sweetest
names coaxed us across to you. Now suddenly
your scent is utter glory in our air.

But even so: We don't know what
to make of it, we speculate . . . and retreat
into nostalgia, invoking inherited hours.

VII

Blumen, ihr schließlich den ordnenden Händen verwandte,
(Händen der Mädchen von einst und jetzt),
die auf dem Gartentisch oft von Kante zu Kante
lagen, ermattet und sanft verletzt,

wartend des Wassers, das sie noch einmal erhole
aus dem begonnenen Tod—, und nun
wieder erhobene zwischen die strömenden Pole
fühlender Finger, die wohlzutun

mehr noch vermögen, als ihr ahntet, ihr leichten,
wenn ihr euch wiederfandet im Krug,
langsam erkühlend und Wärme der Mädchen, wie Beichten,

von euch gebend, wie trübe ermüdende Sünden,
die das Gepflücktsein beging, als Bezug
wieder zu ihnen, die sich euch blühend verbünden.

VII

Flowers: Who finally allow yourselves be used
by arranging hands (girlish hands as often as not)—
Who lay stretched out over the garden table
from edge to edge, exhausted, tenderly wounded,

awaiting the water that revives you one
final time from death already begun—
And now electrified by the sensitive polarity
of sympathetic fingers that help you ever

so much more than you could have suspected,
as you return to your selves in the pitcher,
your fever slowly cooling and exuding

the warmth of young girls like a penitent
confessing dark tiring sins, complicit
in being plucked by your blossoming allies.

VIII

Wenige ihr, der einstigen Kindheit Gespielen
in den zerstreuten Gärten der Stadt:
wie wir uns fanden und uns zögernd gefielen
und, wie das Lamm mit dem redenden Blatt,

sprachen als schweigende. Wenn wir uns einmal freuten,
keinem gehörte es. Wessen wars?
Und wie zergings unter allen den gehenden Leuten
und im Bangen des langen Jahrs.

Wagen umrollten uns fremd, vorübergezogen,
Häuser umstanden uns stark, aber unwahr,—und keines
kannte uns je. Was war wirklich im All?

Nichts. Nur die Bälle. Ihre herrlichen Bogen.
Auch nicht die Kinder ... Aber manchmal trat eines,
ach ein vergehendes, unter den fallenden Ball.

In memoriam, Egon von Rilke

VIII

So few: My one time childhood playmates
in those various city parks. The way
we found and hesitantly liked each other.
And like the little lamb with the talking scroll,

spoke without speaking. Those times we just
exulted—no one of us owned that. Who could?
Or the ways it all fell apart amid the strolling people
and the frightening, slow passing year.

Carriages rolled by, alien, drawn along.
The houses surrounding us were solid but lies.
And no one knew us at all. Was anything real?

Nothing. Just the balls in the air and their masterful arches.
Not even the children... But sometimes, one . . . ah, where
has he vanished? . . . managed to step under that falling ball.

In memoriam, Egon von Rilke

IX

Rühmt euch, ihr Richtenden, nicht der entbehrlichen Folter
und daß das Eisen nicht länger an Hälsen sperrt.
Keins ist gesteigert, kein Herz—, weil ein gewollter
Krampf der Milde euch zarter verzerrt.

Was es durch Zeiten bekam, das schenkt das Schafott
wieder zurück, wie Kinder ihr Spielzeug vom vorig
alten Geburtstag. Ins reine, ins hohe, ins thorig
offene Herz träte er anders, der Gott

wirklicher Milde. Er käme gewaltig und griffe
strahlender um sich, wie Göttliche sind.
Mehr als ein Wind für die großen gesicherten Schiffe.

Weniger nicht, als die heimliche leise Gewahrung,
die uns im Innern schweigend gewinnt
wie ein still spielendes Kind aus unendlicher Paarung.

IX

Judges, don't congratulate yourselves for dispensing
with the rack and the iron collar. Your hearts
haven't made any progress just because
a calculated twinge of mercy makes you grimace.

What it received over time, the scaffold will again
serve up, the way children rediscover
the toys of forgotten birthdays. The god of genuine
mercy would stroll into a pure, lofty, welcoming

heart differently. He'd arrive in a rush of gripping radiance
and bind us to himself, an irresistible divinity.
More than a gale to rock the big unsinkable boats.

Nothing less than the secret sweet recognition
that wordlessly conquers from within
like the quietly playing child of an eternal coupling.

X

Alles Erworbne bedroht die Maschine, solange
sie sich erdreistet, im Geist, statt im Gehorchen, zu sein.
Daß nicht der herrlichen Hand schöneres Zögern mehr prange,
zu dem entschlossenem Bau schneidet sie steifer den Stein.

Nirgends bleibt sie zurück, daß wir ihr ein Mal entrönnen
und sie in stiller Fabrik ölend sich selber gehört.
Sie ist das Leben,—sie meint es am besten zu können,
die mit dem gleichen Entschluß ordnet und schafft und zerstört.

Aber noch ist uns das Dasein verzaubert; an hundert
Stellen ist es noch Ursprung. Ein Spielen von reinen
Kräften, die keiner berührt, der nicht kniet und bewundert.

Worte gehen noch zart am Unsäglichen aus ...
Und die Musik, immer neu, aus den bebendsten Steinen,
baut im unbrauchbaren Raum ihr vergöttlichtes Haus.

X

Because we allow it to exist as *Geist*, no longer an obedient
tool, the machine menaces everything we've gained. It squares
the bricks for our ambitious projects perfectly—just to keep
the master craftsman's hesitant hand from coaxing their

pebbled glow. We've forgotten how to escape it, for once
leave it behind. Even oiling in the stilled factory, it answers
to itself. Usurping life, it knows what's best for us as
it sorts, fabricates and destroys with equal indifference.

When all the while our *being* beckons with graceful
mysteries cascading from a hundred random wellsprings,
a dancing energy at play that makes us genuflect

and wonder. Words that still whisper from things there
aren't words for. Self replenishing music building her
consecrated house of trembling stone in every useless place.

XI

Manche, des Todes, entstand ruhig geordnete Regel,
weiterbezwingender Mensch, seit du im Jägen beharrst;
mehr doch als Falle und Netz, weiß ich dich, Streifen von Segel,
den man hinuntergehängt in den höhligen Karst,

Leise ließ man dich ein, als wärst du ein Zeichen,
Frieden zu feiern. Doch dann: rang dich am Rande der Knecht,
—und, aus den Höhlen, die Nacht warf eine Handvoll von bleichen
taumelnden Tauben ins Licht ...
Aber auch das ist im Recht.

Fern von dem Schauenden sei jeglicher Hauch des Bedauerns,
nicht nur vom Jäger allein, der, was sich zeitig erweist,
wachsam und handelnd vollzieht

Töten ist eine Gestalt unseres wandernden Trauerns....
Rein ist im heiteren Geist,
was an uns selber geschieht.

XI

Roaming, conquering humanity has quietly plotted many a
deadly ruse in the persistent discipline of the hunt. And no trap
or snare more cunning than you—the strip of sailcloth I once
saw lowered into the limestone bird grottoes of Slovenia.

They ever so gently slipped you in as if you were a flag
of truce to cheer. Then, the attendant snapped a corner.
And out of the cavernous night a handful of frenzied gray doves
fluttered into daylight to be shot.
But even *this* is just.

Not the slightest twinge of pity even touches the onlookers,
let alone the hunter who vigilantly dispatches
his efficient, businesslike task.

Killing is another face of our migratory mourning.
Innocently smiling
at what's happened to us.

XII

Wolle die Wandlung. O sei für die Flamme begeistert,
drin sich ein Ding dir entzieht, das mit Verwandlungen prunkt;
jener entwerfende Geist, welcher das Irdische meistert,
liebt in dem Schwung der Figur nichts wie den wendenden Punkt.

Was sich ins Bleiben verschließt, schon ists das Erstarrte;
wähnt es sich sicher im Schutz des unscheinbaren Grau's?
Warte, ein Härtestes warnt aus der Ferne das Harte.
Wehe—: abwesender Hammer holt aus!

Wer sich als Quelle ergießt, den erkennt die Erkennung;
und sie führt ihn entzückt durch das heiter Geschaffne,
das mit Anfang oft schließt und mit Ende beginnt.

Jeder glückliche Raum ist Kind oder Enkel von Trennung,
den sie staunend durchgehn. Und die verwandelte Daphne
will, seit sie lorbeern fühlt, daß du dich wandelst in Wind.

XII

Embrace change. Let yourself be inspired by the very fires
that consume you with their sparkling transformations.
The spirit of renunciation that masters this mortal life ignores
the swinging figure's ups and downs, but loves the turning point.

What's locked in place is numb and congealed.
Are you safe, under that dull gray shell? Just wait:
From somewhere, something even harder warns the petrified
of pain on the way. As a forgotten hammer is poised.

But what about someone who flows from himself like a spring?
Enlightenment enlightens him as she leads him laughing
    through giddy
scenarios, where beginnings may end but endings bring
    beginning.

They're astonished at how every fortunate place their
    travels find
is the child or grandchild of a loss. And shape shifting
    Daphne, as she
feels herself becoming laurel, whispers—I want you to
    change into wind.

XIII

Sei allem Abschied voran, als wäre er hinter
dir, wie der Winter, der eben geht.
Denn unter Wintern ist einer so endlos Winter,
daß, überwinternd, dein Herz überhaupt übersteht.

Sei immer tot in Eurydike—, singender steige,
preisender steige zurück in den reinen Bezug.
Hier, unter Schwindenden, sei, im Reiche der Neige,
sei ein klingendes Glas, das sich im Klang schon zerschlug.

Sei—und wisse zugleich des Nicht-Seins Bedingung,
den unendlichen Grund deiner innigen Schwingung,
daß du sie völlig vollziehst dieses einzige Mal.

Zudemgebrauchten sowohl, wie zum dumpfen und stummen
Vorrat der vollen Natur, den unsäglichen Summen,
zähle dich jubelnd hinzu und vernichte die Zahl.

XIII

Anticipate each goodbye, as if it were
already behind you like a winter that's passed.
Because underneath these winters is such an interminable
winter, that only by hibernating can your heart survive.

Always be dead in Eurydice—climb out the way a singer climbs
in a voice rich with loss and celebration of that pure connection.
And here, below with the ghosts, in the empire of bitter endings
be the clinking glass that, even as it shatters, rings.

Be—and at the same time—realize your inescapable
    nonexistence
is the unquenchable root of your deepest resonance.
And just this once, be all you were meant to become:

To those already used and discarded, and to the numb, mute
stockyard of bloated nature—to that unspeakable sum—
count yourself gladly in and nullify the count.

XIV

Siehe die Blumen, diese dem Irdischen treuen,
denen wir Schicksal vom Rande des Schicksals leihn,—
aber wer weiß es! Wenn sie ihr Welken bereuen,
ist es an uns, ihre Reue zu sein.

Alles will schweben. Da gehn wir umher wie Beschwerer,
legen auf alles uns selbst, vom Gewichte entzückt;
o was sind wir den Dingen für zehrende Lehrer,
weil ihnen ewige Kindheit glückt.

Nähme sie einer ins innige Schlafen und schliefe
tief mit den Dingen—: o wie käme er leicht,
anders zum anderen Tag, aus der gemeinsamen Tiefe

Oder er bliebe vielleicht; und sie blühten und priesen
ihn, den Bekehrten, der nun den Ihringen gleicht,
allen den stillen Geschwistern im Winde der Wiesen.

XIV

Look at the wildflowers so wedded to mortal earth.
We lend them purpose from beyond their
purpose. Who knows if they resent their withering—
or whether it's for us to be their regret?

Everything wants to float. And we go around depressed,
depressing everything—enthralled with gravity.
What exhausting taskmasters we've become
to the eternal childhood of blossoms in their

delight. If someone, somehow took them into intimate
sleep and slept deeply with them—Oh, how easily he'd
awake—new to a new day, out the communal deep.

Or perhaps he'd stay there and they'd bloom
with praise for this convert, now just one of them,
quiet brothers and sisters of the meadow breeze.

XV

O Brunnen-Mund, du gebender, du Mund,
der unerschöpflich Eines, Reines, spricht,—
du, vor des Wassers fließendem Gesicht,
marmorne Maske. Und im Hintergrund

der Aquädukte Herkunft. Weither an
Gräbern vorbei, vom Hang des Apennins
tragen sie dir dein Sagen zu, das dann
am schwarzen Altern deines Kinns

vorüberfällt in das Gefäß davor.
Dies ist das schlafend hingelegte Ohr,
das Marmorohr, in das du immer sprichst.

Ein Ohr der Erde. Nur mit sich allein
redet sie also. Schiebt ein Krug sich ein,
so scheint es ihr, daß du sie unterbrichst.

XV

O fountain-mouth, you benefactor, you
inexhaustible wellspring of crystalline speech—
You're the grinning marble mask of flowing
waters sent from the depths of

the aqueduct's source. From far
away, past ancient ruins and down
the Apennine slopes, your babbling
tumbles over your age blackened

chin out into the basin, the
sound asleep ear, the marble
ear you always converse with,

an ear of the earth, listening
to herself. Slipping in a pitcher,
she's startled by my intrusion.

XVI

Immer wieder von uns aufgerissen,
ist der Gott die Stelle, welche heilt.
Wir sind Scharfe, denn wir wollen wissen,
aber er ist heiter und verteilt.

Selbst die reine, die geweihte Spende
nimmt er anders nicht in seine Welt,
als indem er sich dem freien Ende
unbewegt entgegenstellt.

Nur der Tote trinkt
aus der hier von uns *gehörten* Quelle,
wenn der Gott ihm schweigend winkt, dem Toten.

Uns wird nur das Lärmen angeboten.
Und das Lamm erbittet reine Schelle
Aus dem stilleren Instinkt.

XVI

We scratch at it constantly,
the god, the place which heals.
We're sharp because we want to know
but he's serenely unconcerned.

He accepts even the pure, consecrated
offering indifferently into his world.
And making himself the entrance, he
unmovably blocks all escape.

Only the dead drink from
that wellspring we can only *hear*. When
the god silently winks at the dead.

Only the sound is offered to us.
And something quieter than instinct
moves the lamb to beg for its little bell.

XVII

Wo, in welchen immer selig bewässerten Gärten, an
welchen
Bäumen, aus welchen zärtlich entblätterten Blüten-Kelchen
reifen die fremdartigen Früchte der Tröstung? Diese
köstlichen, deren du eine vielleicht in der zertretenen
Wiese

deiner Armut findest. Von einem zum anderen Male
wundent du dich über die Größe der Frucht,
über ihr Heilsein, über die Sanftheit der Schale,
und daß sie der Leichtsinn des Vogels dir nicht
vorwegnahm und nicht die Eifersucht

unten des Wurms. Gibt es denn Bäume, von Engeln
beflogen,
und von verborgenen langsamen Gärtnern so seltsam
gezogen,
daß sie uns tragen, ohne uns zu gehören?

Haben wir niemals vermocht, wir Schatten und Schemen,
durch unser voreilig reifes und wieder welkes Benehmen
jener gelassenen Sommer Gleichmut zu stören?

XVII

Where, in what forever happy, irrigated grove, on
which tree, and from which gently deflowered calyxes,
do the mysterious fruits of consolation ripen? Those
delicacies you might find dropped into the trampled

meadow of your lack. Over and over, you're
amazed at the size of the fruit, it's soundness
despite its fragile skin. And that some swooping bird
hasn't got to it before you, or the envious worms

from below. Are there trees, then, where angels alight,
secretly tended by unhurried, hidden gardeners, that
bear for us but can never belong to us? Were we ever

capable, we shadows and figments, with our
too quickly ripening, too soon wilting natures,
of disturbing that slow summer's quiet.

XVIII

Tänzerin: O du Verlegung
alles Vergehens in Gang: wie brachtest du's dar.
Und der Wirbel am Schluß, dieser Baum aus Bewegung,
nahm er nicht ganz in Besitz das erschwungene Jahr?

Blühte nicht, daß ihn dein Schwingen von vorhin
        umschwärme,
plötzlich sein Wipfel von Stille? Und über ihr,
war sie nicht Sonne, war sie nicht Sommer, die Wärme,
diese unzählige Wärme aus dir?

Aber er trug auch, er trug, dein Baum der Ekstase.
Sind sie nicht seine ruhigen Früchte: der Krug,
reifend gestreift, und die gereiftere Vase?

Und in den Bildern: ist nicht die Zeichnung geblieben,
die deiner Braue dunkler Zug
rasch an die Wandung der eigenen Wendung geschrieben?

XVIII

Dancer: O how your feet transfigured
everything as it passes, in a veritable tour-de-force.
Your closing whirl, that tree of motion, didn't it
capture the entire slow growing year?

Didn't your cadence suddenly swarm up
and crown it with blossoms of stillness? And above,
wasn't the sun, wasn't summer and its warmth,
your own incalculable warmth.

But it also bore, it bore fruit, your ecstatic tree.
Aren't these its silent fruits: the pitcher
full with ripeness, and an even fuller vase?

And in the photos: doesn't the message remain
that your eyebrows sketched on the blurred
wall of your own pirouette?

XIX

Irgendwo wohnt das Gold in der verwöhnenden Bank,
und mit Tausenden tut es vertraulich. Doch jener
Blinde, der Bettler, ist selbst dem kupfernen Zehner
in verlorener Ort, wie das staubige Eck unterm Schrank.

In den Geschäften entlang ist das Geld wie zuhause
und verkleidet sich scheinbar in Seide, Nelken und Pelz.
Er, der Schweigende, steht in der Atempause
alles des wach oder schlafend atmenden Gelds.

O wie mag sie sich schließen bei Nacht, diese immer offene Hand.
Morgen holt sie das Schicksal wieder, und täglich
hält es sie hin: hell, elend, unendlich zerstörbar.

Daß doch einer, ein Schauender, endlich ihren langen Bestand
staunend begriffe und rühmte. Nur dem Aufsingenden säglich.
Nur dem Göttlichen hörbar.

XIX

Somewhere gold keeps house, in an indulgent
bank, hobnobbing with thousands. But that blind
man begging is as bereft of even one red cent,
as an undusted corner under the dresser.

Clad in silk, carnations and fur, money's
welcomed by all the shops. While *he* waits
in the hush between breaths of all that
waking, sleeping, breathing cash.

Does his always open palm even close at night
before morning arrives compelling it into
light, day after miserable dying day?

If only someone with eyes could grasp the wonder
of that stubborn hand, a poem utterable only
in music that only the god can hear.

XX

Zwischen den Sternen, wie weit; und doch, um wievieles
   noch weiter,
was man am Hiesigen lernt.
Einer, zum Beispiel, ein Kind ... und ein Nächster, ein Zweiter—,
o wie unfaßlich entfernt.

Schicksal, es mißt uns vielleicht mit des Seienden Spanne,
daß es uns fremd erscheint;
denk, wieviel Spannen allein vom Mädchen zum Manne,
wenn es ihn meidet und meint.

Alles ist weit—, und nirgends schließt sich der Kreis.
Sieh in der Schüssel, auf heiter bereitetem Tische,
seltsam der Fische Gesicht.

Fische sind stumm...,
meinte man einmal. Wer weiß?
Aber ist nicht am Ende ein Ort, wo man das, was der Fische
Sprache wäre, *ohne* sie spricht?

XX

What distances separate the stars: but how much more about
distance do we learn from what's close by?
Take a child, for example . . . then the next one, between
the two—an incomprehensible expanse.

Destiny: It takes our measure with a life span
that seems so alien to us. Consider
how much there is to span between a girl and man
when she turns away and thinks about him.

It's all so vast—and the circle doesn't close anywhere.
Look, there in the bowl on the festive table,
at the fish with their strange faces.

Fish are mute . . . Once we were sure. But who knows
if there might yet be somewhere their destined
language is finally spoken *without* them.

XXI

Singe die Gärten, mein Herz, die du nicht kennst; wie in Glas
eingegossene Gärten, klar, unerreichbar.
Wasser und Rosen von Ispahan oder Schiras,
singe sie selig, preise sie, keinem vergleichbar.

Zeige, mein Herz, daß du sie niemals entbehrst.
Daß sie dich meinen, ihre reifenden Feigen.
Daß du mit ihren, zwischen den blühenden Zweigen
wie zum Gesicht gesteigerten Lüften verkehrst.

Meide den Irrtum, daß es Entbehrungen gebe
für den geschehnen Entschluß, diesen: zu sein!
Seidener Faden, kamst du hinein ins Gewebe.

Welchem der Bilder du such im Innern geeint bist
(sei es selbst ein Moment aus dem Leben der Pein),
fühl, daß der ganze, der rühmliche Teppich gemeint ist.

XXI

Sing my heart, your unfound gardens. Terraces
etched in crystal, as clear and unreachable
as water and roses from ancient Persia.
Sing and extol them, blessed, incomparable.

Prove, my heart, you were never
deprived of them. That their ripening figs are
meant for you. How their blossomed
branches greet you with a kiss of breeze.

Resist the illusion of privation. Let yourself
accede to that longed for decision: Just be!
A silken thread woven into the grand design.

Whatever image in it calls you (even if it's
just a moment in a lifetime of grief), feel
how the whole glorious carpet is implicit.

XXII

O trotz Schicksal: die herrlichen Überflüsse
unseres Daseins, in Parken übergeschäumt,—
oder als steinerne Männer neben die Schlüsse
hoher Portale, unter Balkone gebäumt!

O die eherne Glocke, die ihre Keule
täglich wider den stumpfen Alltag hebt.
Oder die *eine*, in Karnak, die Säule, die Säule,
die fast ewige Tempel überlebt.

Heute stürzen die Überschlüsse, dieselben,
nur noch als Eile vorbei, aus dem wagrechten gelben
Tag in die blendend mit Licht übertriebene Nacht.

Aber das Rasen zergeht und läßt keine Spuren.
Kurven des Flugs durch die Luft und die, die sie fuhren,
keine vielleicht ist umsonst. Doch nur wie gedacht.

XXII

Ah, despite our mortality, the glorious froth
of our existence bubbled over and became
parks, or congealed into stone men holding
up balconies under high windows.

O, the bronze bell that clangs its clapper
against the dullness of hourly life. Or
that pillar, the oldest pillar in Karnak still
standing in the almost eternal temple.

In modernity, these effusions just rush
away from our flat yellow days into artificially
dazzling night. Frantic, dissipating without

a trace. Except perhaps the soaring arcs of
airplanes and their stolid pilots. Maybe nothing
really goes to waste, if only in the imagination.

XXIII

Ruft mich zu jener deiner Stunden,
die dir unaufhörlich widersteht:
flehend nah wie das Gesicht von Hunden,
aber immer wieder weggedreht,

wenn du meinst, sie endlich zu erfassen.
So Entzognes ist am meisten dein.
Wir sind frei. Wir wurden dort entlassen,
wo wir meinten, erst begrüßt zu sein.

Bang verlangen wir nach einem Halte,
wir zu Jungen manchmal für das Alte
und zu alt für das, was niemals war.

Wir, gerecht nur, wo wir dennoch preisen,
weil wir, ach, der Ast sind und das Eisen
und das Süße reifender Gefahr.

XXIII

Call me at that hour of yours
that incessantly resists you; begs
you to come closer like the face
of a dog that always escapes again just

when you think you've caught it.
What's most elusive is most yours.
We're free. Dismissed from that place where
we originally thought we were welcome.

Frightened, we grasp for something to hold.
Sometimes we're too young for the ancient
and too old for things that never were.

It's only fitting for us to keep praising,
because, as it is, we're the branch and
the axe and the sweet ripening risk.

XXIV

O diese Lust, immer neu, aus gelockertem Lehm!
Niemand beinah hat den frühesten Wagern geholfen.
Städte entstanden trotzdem an beseligten Golfen,
Wasser und Öl füllten die Krüge trotzdem.

Götter, wir planen sie erst in erkühnten Entwürfen,
die uns das mürrische Schicksal wieder zerstört.
Aber sie sind die Unsterblichen. Sehet, wir dürfen
jenen erhorchen, der uns am Ende erhört.

Wir, ein Geschlecht durch jahrtausende: Mütter und Väter,
immer erfüllter von dem künftigen Kind,
daß es uns einst, übersteigend, erschüttere, später.

Wir, wir unendlich Gewagten, was haben wir Zeit!
Und nur der scheigsame Tod, der weiß, was wir sind
und was er immer gewinnt, wenn er uns leiht.

XXIV

O, the forever fresh urge to break new soil.
The odds were so against those first venturers.
And yet, cities were built on joyous harbors
and urns filled with water and oil.

Early on, we enlisted the gods in bold ploys
that sullen fate snatched from us. But they
remain immortal and we can still patiently
listen for one of their faint distant voices.

Through millennia, we're one generation,
mothers and fathers fulfilled by future children
who shock, then surpass ourselves. Eternal

risk takers, we have so much time to work
with. Only taciturn death knows what we are.
And what, when he lends to us, he earns in return.

XXV

Schon, horch, hörst du der ersten Harken
Arbeit; wieder den menschlichen Takt
in der verhaltenen Stille des starken
Vorfrühlingserde. Unabgeschmackt

scheint dir das Kommende. Jenes so oft
dir schon Gekommene scheint dir zu kommen
wieder wie Neues. Immer erhofft,
nahmst du es niemals. Es hat dich genommen.

Selbst die Blätter durchwinterter Eichen
scheinen im Abend ein künftiges Braun.
Manchmal geben sich Lüfte ein Zeichen.

Schwarz sind die Sträucher. Doch Haufen von Dünger
lagern als satteres Schwarz in den Au'n.
Jede Stunde, die hingeht, wird jünger.

XXV

Listen, you can already hear the first
harrowers at work again. That human pulse
against the resistant hush of the bare, early
spring earth. Something you've yet to taste

is germinating. What's come around so
often, seems completely new. All those
times you yearned for this, you never
captured it. It always captured you.

Tonight, even the budding leaves of
wintered oaks glow in an olive dusk.
Soft gusts whisper and nod. The shrubs

are still black, but heaped fertilizer spreads
its richer black across the open land. Every
hour that passes grows younger.

XXVI

Wie ergreift uns der Vogelschrei...
Irgendein einmal erschaffenes Schreien.
Aber die Kinder schon, spielend im Freien,
schreien an veirklichen Schreien vorbei.

Schreien den Zufall. In Zwischenräume
dieses, des Weltraums, (in welchen der heile
Vogelschrei eingeht, wie Menschen in Träume—)
treiben sie ihre, des Kreischens, Keile.

Wehe, wo sind wir? Immer noch freier,
wie die losgerissenen Drachen
jagen wir halbhoch, mit Rändern von Lachen,

windig zerfetzten.—Ordne die Schreier,
singender Gott! daß sie rauschend erwachen,
tragend als Strömung das Haupt und die Leier.

XXVI

The way we're startled by a bird
screech . . . as with any creature's scream.
But children romping in the open air,
scream something beyond their screams.

Exclaim those spontaneous seams in
the universe (through which bird cries
pass as unhurt as people in dreams)
as they wedge their shrieking way.

Woefully, where are we? Freer and freer
like kites cut loose, we chase around
giggling in mid air, wind-shredded

at the edges. Arrange the criers, singing
god. So they rouse in chorus, a streaming
current carrying your head and lyre.

XXVII

Gibt es wirklich die Zeit, die zerstörende?
Wann, auf dem ruhenden Berg, zerbricht sie die Burg?
Dieses Herz, das unendlich den Göttern gehörende,
wann vergewaltigt's der Demiurg?

Sind wir wirklich so ängstlich Zerbrechliche,
wie das Schicksal uns wahr machen will?
Ist die Kindheit, die tiefe, versprechliche
in den Wurzeln—später—still?

Ach, das Gespenst des Vergänglichen,
durch den arglos Empfänglichen
geht es, als wär es ein Rauch.

Als die, die wir sind, als die Treibenden,
gelten wir doch bei bleibenden
Kräften als göttlicher Brauch.

XXVII

Does time the destroyer truly exist? When
on the quiet mountain does it demolish
its fortress? This heart, forever owned by
the gods, when will the demiurge despoil it?

Are we really so fragile and frightened
as fate would have us? Does all
that deep rooted promise of early
childhood—just petrify?

Ah, for the trusting and receptive
the specter of transience
vanishes like smoke.

And haphazard as we are, we
still matter to enduring powers
as divinity uses us.

XXVIII

O komm und geh, Du, fast noch Kind, ergänze
für einen Augenblick die Tanzfigur
zum reinen Sternbild einer jener Tänze,
darin wir die dumpf ordnende Natur

vergänglich übertreffen. Denn sie regte
sich völlig hörend nur, da Orpheus sang.
Du warst noch die von damals her Bewegte
und leicht befremdet, wenn ein Baum sich lang

besann, mit dir nach dem Gehör zu gehn.
Du wußtest noch die Stelle, wo die Leier
sich tönend hob—; die unerhörte Mitte.

Für sie versuchtest du die schönen Schritte
und hofftest, einmal zu der heilen Feier
des Freundes Gang und Antlitz hinzudrehn.

XXVIII

Oh, turn and turn and add your
still half-child's dancing figure
to the utter constellation of a dance
that for an instant transcends

our cloddish nature: It only rose to true
hearing when Orpheus sang. But you
still danced to that once-upon-a-time,
even a bit annoyed if a tree seemed

slow to attend your impatient ear.
You always understood the lyre's
resonant source—its outrageous heart.

And so you rehearsed lovely steps
hoping to one day guide your friend's
attention to this healing celebration.

     to Vera

XXIX

Stiller Freund der vielen Fernen, fühle,
wie dein Atem noch den Raum vermehrt.
Im Gebälk der finstern Glockenstühle
laß dich läuten. Das, was an dir zehrt,

wird ein Starkes über dieser Nahrung.
Geh in der Verwandlung aus und ein.
Was ist deine leidendste Erfahrung?
Ist dir Trinken bitter, werde Wein.

Sei in dieser Nacht aus Übermaß
Zauberkraft am Kreuzweg deiner Sinne,
ihrer seltsamen Begegnung Sinn.

Und wenn dich das Irdische vergaß,
zu der stillen Erde sag: Ich rinne.
Zu dem raschen Wasser sprich: Ich bin.

XXIX

Silent friend of so much wandering, feel
how your breath still creates new
spaces. From the rafters of dark belfries,
let yourself ring. What feeds on you is

nourished, grows strong with you.
Accept and join that transformation.
What brings you your deepest pain?
If that cup is bitter, become the wine.

At the crossroads of this overwhelming
night be the sorcerer and spell, the catalyst
of your being's uncanny convergence.

And if what's earthly forgets you,
remind the silent earth: I flow.
Tell the hurrying water: I am.

To Vera's friend

AND YET ANOTHER
ARCHAIC TORSO—WHY?

A version of this article originally appeared in Jacket Magazine *in 2008. It's appended here not as a critique or an exercise in comparative translation, but primarily as an example of the kind of energies that impel retranslation of iconic works—as much a twelve-year-earlier prequel as an afterword to this volume.*

I. A Compendium of Voices

At the 1999 American Literary Translators Association conference in New York City, Rainer Schulte commented that despite dozens of versions, Americans continue to retranslate Rilke and would probably keep on doing so until "we finally get it right."

1999 was also the year that William Gass's *Reading Rilke* appeared. For those who haven't read that book, it contains not only Gass's translations of the *Duino Elegies* but extensive discussion on and comparative translations of a number of other Rilke poems. The cumulative result seems to be a compendium of voices that, taken together, might be thought to approximate and recreate Rilke's voice in English.

Gass's book seemed almost universally well received and reviewed. The only (partial) dissent I've come across is an essay by Marjorie Perloff—*Reading Gass Reading Rilke*, originally published in *Parnassus,* but now readily available on the internet.

While Perloff gives Gass full credit for his critical acuity, she also notes—as a native speaker—the "clunkiness" of Gass's translation choices (and of many of the comparative translation quotes). I'm wary of oversimplifying a nuanced and informative essay that rewards a full reading. But as I read her, Perloff might be characterized as saying that while Gass's critical and biographical insights are often wonderful, the actual translations seem to fail to capture the unique and subtle combination of modernism, animism, and poetic abstraction that Gass's critique so aptly describes. She also notes—as other native speakers do—that for all his complexity, Rilke's German voice in the *Elegies* remains conversational and contemporary, unlike the highly mannered, "high poetic" tone of many of the translations.

II. High Poetics

As a native English speaker, my own observation is that I'm struck by how commonplace it is for Rilke translators to comment on Rilke's "lack of a sense of humor." Most translators also seem unwilling to be open to any ironic interpretations in Rilke. For these translators, high poetics will consistently trump irony. I think Gass exemplifies this approach in a chapter entitled "Ein Gott Vermags" that discusses translating the "First Duino Elegy." He compares fourteen versions of the poem's opening lines:

> Wer, wenn ich schrie, hörte mich denn aus der Engel
> Ordungen? Und gesetzt selbst, es nähme
> einer mich plötzlich ans Herz: ich verginge von seinem
> stärken Dasein, Denn das Schöne ist nichts
> als des Schrecklichen Anfang, den wir noch grade ertragen,
> und wir bewundern es so, weil es gelassen verschmäht,
> und zu zerstören. Ein jeder Engel ist schrecklich.

Gass finds most versions insufficiently poetic for
various reasons but manages to stitch together his
version with the help of the others:

> Who, if I cried, would hear me among the Dominions
> of Angels? And if one of them suddenly held me
> against his heart, I would fade in the grip
> of that completer existence—beauty we can barely
> endure, because it is nothing but terror's herald;
> and we worship it so because it serenely disdains
> to destroy us. Every Angel is awesome.

To translate these opening lines is admittedly a serious
task. They're as famous as the opening of *The Waste
Land*. In fact, I think there are many parallels between
the "First Elegy," written in 1912, and Eliot's *The Waste
Land*, published ten years later. For one, there is the
theme of facing existential issues without being able
to access the traditional comforts that lie in ruins—
writing from a crack in the order of things. Eliot's
poem is set in the aftermath of World War I; Rilke's,
almost eerily, foreshadows that cataclysm. "First Elegy"
begins with a sense of vague foreboding, and weighs
and discards one explanation after another until the
elegy settles on what's arguably its central image:
"those dead youths" "taken before their time." Their
very names "tossed aside like broken toys."

And, for me, another similarity is the sense of barely
controlled neurosis that *The Waste Land* subtly
begins to assume as it slips into the voice of the
Countess Marie. Somewhere around the tenth line,
The Waste Land's meter begins to take on a nervous
heartbeat:

> And went on in sunlight, into the Hofgarten,
> And drank coffee, and talked for an hour.

Bin gar keine Russin, stamm' aus Litauen, echt deutsch.
And when we were children, staying at the archduke's,
My cousin's, he took me out on a sled,
And I was frightened. He said, Marie,
Marie, hold on tight. And down we went.

I get this same sense at the beginning (but not the
end) of the "First Elegy." The initial images may be
exalting for some, but they could also be discussion
points for an analyst's session. The "cunning
animals" who "notice the world's a language in
which we're not always quite at home." "Night,
when the wind full of outer space feeds on our
faces." For me, the *schrie* isn't a "cry" or a "call," but
something closer to the Edvard Munch *Scream*.
And to my ear, Gass's version of these lines reads
not as particularly poetic but as something like
CliffsNotes for readers with a nineteenth-century
aesthetic trying to digest a modernist poem. Rilke
translated by Wordsworth.

Gass seems particularly disdainful of the
conversational tone of David Young's version:

If I cried out
who would hear me up there
among the angelic orders?

And suppose one suddenly
took me to his heart.
I would shrivel

I couldn't survive
next to his
greater existence.

Beauty is only the first touch of terror we
can still bear and it awes us so much
because it so coolly disdains to destroy us.

Every single angel is terrible.

I've always liked Young's version, and I'd be
tempted to take that wry intimate voice farther in
English, even bordering on idiom:

Then even if I screamed to high heaven, who'd listen
to me there among the angelic orders? And
suppose one of them did swoop me to heart:
I'd die, seared by exposure to that stark, concentrated
being. Because beauty's nothing, the mere beginning
of a panic we're still just barely able to contain.
And we continually praise it, hoping it continues
to disdainfully refrain from obliterating us.
Every one of the angels is terrifying.

III. Workshopping

As someone who's been translating Rilke on and
off for years, my own reaction on reading Gass
was: "Well that's it! The last nail in the coffin." Gass
seemed to present such a comprehensive picture of
what's out there—the agreed upon, standard Rilke,
as it were—that Rilke's English voice seemed gelled
for our time. It seemed to me, after reading Gass
and his reviewers, that it was going to take another
generation before anyone might be open to anything
significantly different.

But why do I think the "standard" Rilke voice—
the one that seems to be shared by most of the
ubiquitous versions—*needs* a new generation of

translators? I've always felt that Rilke stands with one foot in the nineteenth century with the other firmly planted in the twenty-first. I've sometimes thought of him, especially in the *Elegies*, as the poetic leg of a three-legged stool—the other two legs being Einstein and Freud / Jung.

To my mind, the current trend in translating these essentially modern—maybe even still emergent— poems is that translators seem to be insistent on falling back into the nineteenth century rather than to where Rilke's unique aesthetic is leading us. Or maybe more appropriately—where that aesthetic might lead us after taking on a second life in English. Because insofar as poetic translation is poetry, it's an exploration of the target rather than the source language.

I began translating Rilke in the 1970s. At the time, Rilke wasn't the icon in America he's since become. (Did Rilke's "American—Idolization" begin sometime in the 1980s when, in the deal of the century, we seem to have traded Bukowski to Germany for Rilke?) The translations I was aware of were Herter Norton's and MacIntyre's and a few others dating from the 1930s and '40s. But this was also the time that David Young's iconoclastic translations of the *Duino Elegies* began coming out in *Field*. They spoke in an immediate, contemporary English voice. I've often felt that the open form of the *Elegies* makes their poetry more, not less, difficult to capture. Young recast the *Elegies* in William Carlos Williams-like triplets that seemed to energize and focus the rambling poems. This was a poet I didn't recognize in Norton or MacIntyre. So I started playing with translating Rilke on my own. Above all, I wanted to hang onto that "twenty-first-century leg."

Robert Bly was also publishing his highly personalized Rilke versions, and though some of these have been since maligned, many have an energy and stand on their own as poems in English. They contained qualities shared by Lowell's very loose "imitations." These are qualities, I think, often lacking in the trend that started with the "more accurate" Mitchell.

The scope of Stephen Mitchell's contribution— both in interpreting and popularizing Rilke is unquestioned. But since Mitchell, the trend, to me at least, seems to involve less an internalization and rerendering of the original text than a retranslation of existing translations, with Gass—in some cases, blatantly patchwork versions—representing a kind of translation by committee culmination.

It's as if Rilke (or Mitchell) has been "workshopped." To my taste, so many of the recent versions seem akin to the "translation" of German craft beer into Budweiser. Or of *terroir*-driven wine traditions into the Mondovino international style. The current translations are popular, accessible, and retain an underlying Rilke spirit that can still at times intoxicate.

But for the most part, at least for me, they fall short of that rare but essential poetic translation quality: the ability to be read as if they were originally written in the target language. They remain not poems but representations of poems. Above all they seem to lack the element of risk that—like flight—poetic translation demands.

IV. An Aesthetic Question

So, at the risk of setting myself up for a great pratfall—let me try to demonstrate some of what

I think is lacking. "Archaic Torso of Apollo" is
a ubiquitously translated chestnut that I think
provides a good forum for the kind of dialogue that
might be productive.

Archaischer Torso Apollos

Wir kannten nicht sein unerhörtes Haupt,
darin die Augenäpfel reiften. Aber

sein Torso glüht noch wie ein Kandelaber,
in dem sein Schauen, nur zurückgeschraubt,

sich hält und glänzt. Sonst könnte nicht der Bug,
der Brust dich blenden, und im leisen Drehen
der Lenden könnte nicht ein Lächeln gehen
zu jener Mitte, die die Zeugung trug.

Sonst stünde dieser Stein entstellt und kurz
unter der Schultern durchsichtigem Sturz
und flimmerte nicht so wie Raubtierfelle

und bräche nicht aus allen seinen Rändern
aus wie ein Stern: denn da ist keine Stelle,
die dich nicht sieht. Du mußt dein Leben ändern.

What follows is my own most recent version (2007)—
maybe the twentieth revision in as many years and
almost certainly not the final version.

Archaic Torso of Apollo

We didn't understand that outrageous head, the eyes
whose irises actually flowered. But his torso
still stares like a chandelier turned low,
dimmed to illuminate just its own steady

flame. Why else would the crease
of the chest muscles blind you? And the slight
tensing of the loin—it's nothing if not a smile
traveling to his center on a journey to procreation.

If not, this would only be a fragment
of mutilated stone under the shoulders' transparent
slump. Wouldn't glisten, anymore than a predator's

fur, or leap like radiating star fire.
Because there isn't any single part of it that isn't
watching you. You have to live another life.

My fear of a pratfall is triggered from line one here.
Let me preface with the admission that I have very
limited confidence in my entry-level German. But I
do rely heavily on my own sense of what constitutes
the "poetic" and on my own, perhaps quirky, sense of
Rilke's aesthetic. Querying native speakers is always
invaluable, but Rilke's multilevel images seem to lead
even the German reader to the realm of questions
that belie final answers.

So what makes me so brash as to diverge from almost
every American translator's reading of the first
sentence? *Wir kannten nicht sein unerhörtes Haupt,
darin die Augenäpfel reiften.* In her 1938 volume,
Norton translated the lines as follows:

We did not know his legendary head,
in which the eyeballs ripened.

Mitchell, in what's arguably the "standard"
contemporary collection, in 1984:

We cannot know his legendary head
with eyes like ripening fruit.

Snow's 1987 version:

> We never knew his head and all the light
> that ripened in his fabled eyes.

And Gass, in 1999.

> Never will we know his legendary head
> where the eye's apples slowly ripened.

Rilke refers to the statue's missing head as *unerhörtes*. I've yet to find a German dictionary (or native speaker) that doesn't define *unerhörtes* as some variant of "outrageous," generally with a negative implication. The word literally means "unheard of," but can also be applied to a "fabulous price." Norton notes that she moved it along from "fabulous" to "legendary." As can be seen above, nearly everyone seems to have followed her lead, and given that her German was probably better than mine and she was closer to Rilke's time, she may well be right.

But, there are aesthetic consequences. *Augenäpfel* is literally German for "eyeballs." In choosing between "outrageous" or "legendary" for *unerhörtes*, you have to ask whether Rilke meant the next phrase— *augenäpfel reiften* ("eye-apples ripened")—to be a gently eye-ball rolling pun or a serious poetic image.

Because that interpretative choice—coming as it does in the very first line—effectively moves the poem either forward or backward in time. Is this 1908 poem an early modernist poem—a "New Poem"—or a piece that begins by invoking a nineteenth-century nostalgia?

In a 2007 *New Yorker* article, Milan Kundera returns to a favorite subject—"kitsch." A word, he says, that "describes the syrupy dregs of the great Romantic period." He goes on to say that "Kitsch long ago became a very precise concept in Central Europe, where it represents the supreme aesthetic evil." His references are somewhat later than 1908, when "Archaic Torso" was published, but it's hard for me to accept that

Rilke—a contemporary of Kafka and Kockoschka, a late Austrian Empire sophisticate, and an emerging modernist—would, at this stage in his career, treat *augenäpfel reiften* as a totally serious image. Doesn't *unerhörtes*, when literally translated, reinforce this? And doesn't stretching the standard context of *unerhörtes* into "fabled" or "legendary"—into something positive rather than negative or suspect— just add to the kitsch?

V. Back to the Future?

If we back away a bit and put "Archaic Torso" into its publication context, maybe the translation choice can be clarified. "Archaic Torso" is the first piece in the second volume (or as titled "Another Part") of *New Poems*. The first volume, released in 1907, begins with another Apollo poem—"Früher Apollo" (Early—or childhood—Apollo). That poem begins:

Wie manches Mal durch das noch unbelaubte
Gezweig ein Morgen durchsieht, der schon ganz
im Frühling ist: so ist in seinem Haupte
nichts, was verhindern könnte, dass der Glanz

aller Gedichte uns fast tödlich träfe;
denn noch kein Schatten ist in seinem Schaun,

Roughly:

> The same way once in a while through the still
> bare branches a morning glares through that's already
> entirely spring; that's the way there's nothing
> in his head to prevent it: The brilliance
>
> of all poems from searing us almost fatally.
> Because there's nothing to shade us from his stare . . .

The poem goes on to say that "only later" would the
child Apollo's eyebrows sprout up into a tall rose
garden from which the petals would drop "into his
trembling mouth," as if his songs were being instilled
in him. Quite an "outrageous" head.

Snow, in his preface to *New Poems, 1908. The
Other Part,* compares the two Apollo "frontispiece"
poems. He quotes Rilke's letter to his publisher that
expressed the hope that the second volume could
chart a somewhat parallel course with the first,
but "only somewhat higher, and at a greater depth
and with more distance." If so, might Rilke—in
beginning *New Poems, Another Part*—be saying: "This
is where we came from but not where we're going." It
may be clear poetic logic for the Apollo frontispiece
of the second volume to begin by distinguishing itself
from the first Apollo with a wry pun. But beyond
that, the dismissive *unerhörtes* allows Rilke to have
it both ways—to both acknowledge and incorporate
the pun as an essential element of the poem.

My own (still somewhat clumsy) choice for the first
sentence of "Archaic Torso" would be something
like: "We didn't understand that outrageous head,
those eyes whose irises actually flowered." But in
any case, I don't think "Archaic Torso" should be

translated without keeping "Infant Apollo" in mind as a touchstone. So much has been written in English about what "Archaic Torso" means, but very little about what it "says." Referencing "Infant Apollo" helps ground us from endless philosophizing.

VI. The Candelabrum

While *unerhörtes* in the first sentence has been treated fairly uniformly by most translators, *Kandelaber* in the second sentence has been a subject of some controversy. In his commentary on this poem, Gass summarizes the discourse. He notes that Herter Norton interprets the second sentence as: "But his torso still glows like a candelabrum in which his gaze, only turned low, holds and gleams."

But Leishman, another early Rilke translator, said that *Kandelaber* was, at the time, colloquial for a gas street lamp. Leishman's translation reads: "his torso like a branching street lamp's glowing wherein his gaze, only turned down, can shed light still." Gass expands on the street lamp image: "Yet his torso glows as if his looks were set above it in suspended globes that shed a street's light down."

The difficulty here, I think, is the compound word *zurückgeschraubt*, literally "back screwed" or "screwed down"—a mechanical word that doesn't seem to appropriately modify either candlelight or a gaze. But the problem with the streetlamp image is twofold. For one thing, gas streetlamps are either lit or unlit—all the way on or all the way off. Secondly, the streetlamp image seems to come from somewhere outside the poem, somewhere more Cocteau surreal than Rilkean. What's a streetlamp doing in a museum, and why is Apollo lounging against it?

This sentence seems to give everyone fits. Both Mitchell and Willis Barnstone (in a fairly newly published translation) seem to do as well as anyone in making sense of it. Mitchell: "And yet his torso is still suffused with brilliance from inside, like a lamp, in which his gaze, now turned to low, gleams in all its power." Barnstone: "Yet his torso still glows like a candelabra turned low in which his inner gaze is never dead and gleams with power."

But the image still seems blurred, wordy, and somehow a "reach." How do you turn a candelabra low? And Mitchell's image evokes an oil or kerosene lamp, not a multiflamed candelabra. He makes up for the diminished flame by interjecting "in all its power." And is it a sign of how "standard" Mitchell's 1980's versions have become that Barnstone also interjects "power"?

When I first tried to translate "Archaic Torso" in the 1970s, I had similar problems understanding the image and simply chose to slough it off with an imagined spin: "But his torso still glows as if it were a candelabrum held out—tentative and brilliant—in front of himself to light the way." I can only attempt to pardon myself by noting that my own spin was probably no more fanciful than Gass's or Leishman's. But by the time I revisited the poem in the late 1990s, I was lucky enough to have come across a tattered Rilke contemporary Hachette German-English dictionary at a garage sale. Lo and behold, unlike most current dictionaries, that circa 1910 dictionary contains only one definition for *Kandelaber*— chandelier!

So Leishman was at least half right. This poem dates not from the era of candlelight and oil lamps but from the end of the gaslight era, when even the first electric chandeliers were produced with alternate gas jets to hedge the emerging technology bet. And the regulating screw of the gas chandelier preceded its modern counterpart—the dimmer switch. There are antique "candelabra chandeliers" for sale on the internet, and my sense is that, at least in English candelabra and chandelier, the two words were probably more or less interchangeable until the language chose chandelier for electric fixtures and (as in German) relegated candelabra to candle light.

My own current version is:

But his torso
  still stares like a chandelier turned low,
    dimmed to illuminate just its own steady / flame.

You could legitimately question whether "stare" is too strong a word for *Schauen* (a noun in the original). But looking at this poem in tandem with "Infant Apollo," "stare" is certainly not too strong for the word *Schaun* in the line quoted above: *denn noch kein Schatten ist ein seinem Schaun*—a look containing the brilliance of all poems, and capable of fatally searing us.

VII. The Decapitated God

Now, I have to beg forbearance if I edge into the territory of what the poem "means" as opposed to what it "says." My intent isn't philosophical, but aesthetic—to explore the emotional tone of the images.

New Poems includes four on the theme of Christ's crucifixion, including, in the 1907 volume, "The Garden of Olives" and the wonderful "Pietà," in which Magdalene rather than the Blessed Mother cradles Christ's body and laments the sex they never had. These are paralleled in the 1908 "Another Part" by the starkly naturalistic, almost clinical "Crucifixion," followed by "The Risen," in which Magdalene confronts her still quite complicated would-be lover's feelings in a poem in which it's left for the reader to infer whether it's Christ or Magdalene who's resurrected.

I may be reading too much into "Archaic Torso" (if too much is ever possible in this piece), but as I get to the second stanza, a mental image of the Apollonian equivalent of a church altar crucifix begins to form. Why is Apollo's head missing?

Whether deliberately decapitated or just neglected, the god has been desecrated and sacrificed. The stone is inhabited, alive with meaning, and almost every one of the lines could be applied to the way a believer might view a figure of the crucified Christ. (As a parallel, the child Apollo in "Infant Apollo" might as easily evoke the Christ Child).

The "procreative smile" might seem blasphemous or sadistic in a crucifixion scene, but Baudelaire or Rimbaud wouldn't flinch, and what makes this Apollonian instead of Christian is that we have the semen-smile in place of redemptive blood. (As an aside, there's also a smile in the last stanza of "Infant Apollo": *und nur mit seinem Lächeln etwas trinkend*; "and only with his smile does he drink these things")

But to get back to the point: Just as the torso's powerful *Schauen* in the second sentence flows from the tricky *Augenapfel* in the first line, the failure to acknowledge divinity, with which the poem opens, echoes its consequences in the mutilated stone (*enstellt und kurz*). In fact the opening words, *Wir kannten nicht*, translated in their German word order are "We knew not," evocative of the biblical "Father forgive them for they know not what they do."

This is another reason I find myself departing from the same kind of easy romanticism that delights in fabled ripening eye apples. *New Poems*, especially the 1908 volume, contain a plethora of starkly etched images and pieces like "Corpse Washing" and "The Beggars." "Archaic Torso," for all its animism, seems no less stark.

At the risk of belaboring the impact of that small opening adjective, if we briefly return to *unerhörtes* in the first line, it's interesting to note that my early twentieth-century Hachette also includes in its definitions of that word an official dismissive: "refused, not granted," adding another layer of meaning to the dismissed head—and the rejected god we didn't understand.

But when you start off with a "legendary" head, one can understand how a translator might find it appropriate to poeticize Apollo's shoulders in *dieser Stein enstellt und kurz unter den Schultern durchsichtigem Sturz.*

Norton did: "Else would this stone be standing maimed and short under the shoulders' translucent plunge."

Mitchell, expanding her lead, says: "Otherwise this stone would seem defaced beneath the translucent cascade of the shoulders."

Not to mention Gass: "Otherwise this stone would not be so complete from its shoulder showering body into absent feet."

Somehow, although he reaches pretty far for the sake of a rhyme ("knife" to go with "life" in the sonnet's final line), Willis Barnstone presents an image more consistent with the headless god: "Without that light this stone would have no face, its falling shoulders crack loose with knife."

Perhaps, I'm too drawn to a more conversational voice here, but I find what seems an unembellished translation of *Schultern durchsictigen Sturz* into where it seems to want to go in roughly idiomatic English is sufficient in itself: i.e., the "shoulders' transparent slump."

The god, after all, has been rejected—not to mention decapitated. How did the translucent waterfalls get in here? An image that seems to have no connection with either the stone or the inhabitant god.

It's worth noting that Snow, departing from the "cascade," reads the line as "shoulders' invisible plunge." An abstract image that—while triggering the question: "What's an invisible plunge?"—at least points to an invisible inhabitant.

VIII. Tiger, Tiger Burning Bright

For me the poem's most difficult images are the ones that follow the slumping shoulders: *und flimmerte nicht so wie Raubtierfelle; / und bräche nicht aus allen Rändern / aus wie ein Stern.* Literally "and not glitter the way a predator's fur, and not break out from every boundary the way a star."

Is there an implied double negative here? *Raubtier* is the only generalized or abstract noun in the poem, a class of beasts rather than a particular animal. (The *Raubtierhaus* in the zoo, like the "Lion House" holds a variety of big cats.) And *Stern*, here, also seems to have as much to do with the concept of stars as with any particular star.

What nags at me, attempting to translate these lines, is that predators' coats don't glitter—they're camouflaged, so they generally blend with the landscape. Night hunting cats slink in the shadows. It's only in poetry

that tigers burn bright in the night. Similarly, bursting stars are a rarity. The power of a star is generally self-contained. And even if one broods on black holes and light years, an actual starburst is a remote, cool and silent omen having no discernible connection with ferocious animals.

When I first attempted this poem in the 1970s, I presumed way too much liberty and recklessly recast the lines as: "and shed no more light than the coats of night hunting beasts, couldn't break out of itself anymore than the power of a star from its gravity."

When I returned to the "Torso" twenty years later, I decided this was far too much spin. After all, a big cat in the mind's eye can glitter the way, say, a roll of fifty dollar bills "glitters" or a cartoon fire cracker "shimmers." And if Rilke's "Panther" were ever to break free of its cage, might it not be like an exploding star?

But I'm still not happy with my current version: "Wouldn't glisten, anymore than a predator's fur, or leap like radiating star fire." I sense I'm not catching some very simple possibility that might retain the sense of both abstraction and compressed dangerous energy these lines seem to have in German, but which seems to dissipate in most English versions.

IX. Another Life

The last line of "Archaic Torso," *Du mußt dein Leben ändern*, has probably generated as much philosophic commentary as any line in twentieth-century poetry. Perhaps because, at least in English translation, it seems to come from nowhere. A tiger's leap of a conclusion: "You have to change your life."

A simple, conversational statement, but readers, translators, and commentators seem to agree it means something deeper than "You need a new job" or "It's time for divorce." Interpretations abound and it would be nice to have fifty dollars for every academic essay and term paper written about this line.

Almost all translators have recognized the need to read more weight into the line than "you need a change," and most have reinforced this by using "*must* change" rather than the conversational "have to" or "need to" change. But no one—at least no contemporary poet—would say "you *must* change" in current American usage. Using "*must*" interjects at best an Anglicized voice, but also to American ears a consciously Victorian tone. Rather than an insistent inner whisper in a museum, *"must"* imparts a proclamation in an artificial voice. Yet even the literal, conversational *"you have to change your life"* startles the reader and sends critical commentators into the realms of uncharted metaphysics.

But what if the line doesn't quite come out of nowhere? Maybe it would be helpful to think about this line not just "philosophically" but like a poet publishing the second volume of *New Poems*. A volume that Rilke titled, not Part Two—that would imply just a continuation of the theme—but rather *Der neuen Gedichte anderer Teil* or *New Poems: Another Part*.

In German, to change your life is to "other" your life. So there's not a great verbal leap from the title page *"anderer Teil"* (Another Part) to *"dein Leben ändern"* (change your life). It's not hard to imagine a poet mulling the frontispiece to his second volume by thinking: You have to not just a second volume, but a whole new start. You have to live another life.

Which came first—another life or another part? It doesn't really matter. But I think *Du müßt dein Leben ändern* and *Der . . . anderer Teil* echo and give weight to each other. And the correspondence shouldn't be ignored.

X. Why?

The Rilke canon is particularly rich and varied. He presents us with a multitude of almost contradictory voices: the modernist nonbeliever capable of projecting himself into the reverence of the Book

of Hours, or The Life of Mary; the stark naturalist
of The Voices able to speak in the unadorned
voice of a person suicidal, a drunkard, a beggar;
the early formalist and the narrative master; the
philosophical imagist of the *Elegies*; the ephemeral
musician of the *Sonnets to Orpheus*. Rilke's broad
range and multiple personalities require multiple
translators. It would take another Rilke to have the
skills to tackle it all.

Beyond this, some of the individual poems—
especially the *Elegies* and *Sonnets to Orpheus* have a
complexity of resonance and ambiguity that calls out
for multiple interpretations. Perhaps "performance"
is a better word for what a "poetic" translation of
these poems demands. And if the objective is to
enrich the English language, then there's room for as
many performances of Rilke as, say, interpretations
of Bach. These might be as varied as Wanda
Landowska's, Glenn Gould's, Stefan Hussong's, and
John Lewis's—while remaining as recognizably
Rilke as those versions remain essentially Bach.
It's not hard to imagine Bach relaxing with the
angels, listening to the hundreds of versions and
transcriptions, and smiling. "Wow, look what they've
done with my song." Might we allow ourselves to
imagine something similar with Rilke?

So what's the conclusion? Yes, I think multilayered,
complex poets like Rilke do need to be retranslated
almost continually, not especially until we "get it
right." That's just a beginning because language
lives and changes, and poems written a hundred or
a thousand years ago can only come alive for the
first time again in a new language. German has only
one Rilke, but we can find fresh Rilkes in every new

generation, as long as translators return to the text—
and themselves—rather than their predecessors.

But—and this is a big question—Rilke may now well
be the most popular foreign language poet in the
English-speaking world. And if it's his "standard"
translated voice that people love, why would anyone
want anything different? Do we, in fact, have to
wait another twenty years or so for the current icon
to go out of fashion before anyone will accept a
contrary look? That's why I feel compelled to provide
this commentary rather than just publishing the
translation and being done with it.

The Translator

Art **Beck** is a poet, essayist, and translator whose work has appeared in book and magazine form since the early 1970s. His *Opera Omnia Or, a Duet for Sitar and Trombone*, versions of the sixth-century CE North African Roman poet Luxorius (Otis Books/Seismicity Editions, 2013), won the 2013 Northern California Book Award for translated poetry. *Mea Roma*, a 140-poem "meditative sampling" of Martial's epigrams, was published by Shearsman Books in 2018, and was also awarded Honorable Mention in the American Literary Translators Association 2018 Cliff Becker Prize. In 2019, his poetic sequence *The Insistent Island* was published by Magra Books in its annual chapbook series. From 2009 through 2012, Beck was a regular contributor to *Rattle*, with essays on translating poetry under the rubric "The Impertinent Duet." His articles on the translator's art have appeared in *Jacket2, Your Impossible Voice, The Journal of Poetics Research, PN Review* and *The Los Angeles Review of Books*. He makes his home in San Francisco.

SHANTI ARTS

NATURE ▪ ART ▪ SPIRIT

Please visit us online
to browse our entire book
catalog, including poetry
collections and fiction, books
on travel, nature, healing, art,
photography, and more.

Also take a look at our highly
regarded art and literary journal,
Still Point Arts Quarterly, which
may be downloaded for free.

WWW.SHANTIARTS.COM